ANNUAL REPORT BOOKLET

TO ACCOMPANY

D1291906

SIXTH EDITION

SIXTH EDITION

ACCOUNTING

A BUSINESS PERSPECTIVE

FINANCIAL ACCOUNTING

A BUSINESS PERSPECTIVE

ROGER H. HERMANSON, PH.D., CPA
Regents Professor of Accounting
Ernst & Young–J.W. Hollaway Memorial Professor
School of Accountancy
Georgia State University

JAMES DON EDWARDS, PH.D., CPA
J.M. Tull Professor of Accounting
J.M. Tull School of Accounting
University of Georgia

MICHAEL W. MAHER, PH.D., CPA
Graduate School of Management
University of California at Davis

ROGER H. HERMANSON, PH.D., CPA
Regents Professor of Accounting
Ernst & Young–J.W. Hollaway Memorial Professor
School of Accountancy
Georgia State University

JAMES DON EDWARDS, PH.D., CPA
J.M. Tull Professor of Accounting
J.M. Tull School of Accounting
University of Georgia

IRWIN

Chicago • Bogotá • Boston • Buenos Aires • Caracas
London • Madrid • Mexico City • Sydney • Toronto

PREFACE

Have you ever held stock in a company? If so, you have probably received the company's annual report. Unless you have an accounting background, you would have difficulty understanding its content and using it to make business decisions.

This Annual Report Booklet contains portions of the 1993 annual reports of four actual companies. The companies are The Coca-Cola Company, John H. Harland Company, The Limited, Inc., and Maytag Corporation. Stockholders of these companies all received copies of the annual report. Although you may have heard of some or all of these companies, it may be useful to read a short description of each company.

The Coca-Cola Company is the largest manufacturer, marketer, and distributor of soft drink concentrates and syrups in the world. The company is also the largest marketer of juice and juice-drink products in both the United States and the world.

John H. Harland Company is the nation's second largest check printing company. The company also offers business services and innovative financial solutions to its customers.

The Limited, Inc., is a large merchandiser of women's, men's, and children's apparel. As of 1993, the company had 4,623 stores in the United States under various names, such as Express, Lerner New York, The Limited, and Victoria's Secret Stores.

Magtag Corporation is a leading appliance enterprise focused on five principle areas of home management: laundry, cooking, dishwashing, refrigeration, and floor care. The corporation's appliance brands include Maytag, Hoover, Jenn-Air, Magic Chef, and Admiral. Dixie-Narco is the corporation's vending equipment manufacturer.

HOW TO USE THIS BOOKLET

Many of the questions, exercises, and business decision cases in the text are based on the annual reports contained in this booklet. By the time you are required to respond to these items you will have acquired the knowledge to do so. You will be told where to find the required information in this booklet.

We hope that by using the annual reports of actual companies you will be abe to analyze annual reports of other companies in which you may eventually hold stock. Be sure to have this booklet handy when you are working the end of chapter items. Good luck and have fun.

The Authors

ISBN 0-256-17913-4
© RICHARD D. IRWIN, INC., 1995
Printed in the United States of America
1 2 3 4 5 6 7 8 9 ML 0 9 8 7 6 5 4

The Coca-Cola Company and Subsidiaries

FINANCIAL REVIEW INCORPORATING
MANAGEMENT'S DISCUSSION AND ANALYSIS

Management's primary objective is to maximize share-owner value over time. To accomplish this objective, The Coca-Cola Company and subsidiaries (the Company) have developed a comprehensive business strategy that emphasizes maximizing long-term cash flows. This strategy focuses on continuing aggressive investment in the high-return soft drink business, increasing returns on existing investments and optimizing the cost of capital through appropriate financial policies. The success of this strategy is evidenced by the growth in the Company's cash flows and earnings, its increased returns on total capital and equity and the total return to its share owners over time.

Investments

The Company has a global business system which distributes its products in more than 195 countries. With this pervasive global business system in place, the Company is well positioned to capitalize on new investment opportunities as they arise. Within the last two years, the Company has gained entry into several countries, such as Romania and India. The Company has also rapidly expanded its system across relatively untapped markets such as China, East Central Europe and Indonesia.

Management seeks investments that strategically enhance existing operations and offer cash returns that exceed the Company's long-term after-tax weighted average cost of capital, estimated by management to be approximately 11 percent as of January 1, 1994. The Company's soft drink business generates inherent high returns on capital, providing an attractive area for continued investment. With international per capita consumption of Company products at only 11 percent of the U.S. level, attractive investment opportunities exist in many international markets for the Company and its bottlers to expand production and distribution systems. Even in countries such as the United States, which have more developed soft drink markets, additional high-return investments can be made to increase product choices and availability, enhance marketing focus and improve overall efficiency. The Company has already benefited from the continued consolidation of production and distribution networks, plus investment in the latest technology and information systems.

Capital expenditures on property, plant and equipment and the percentage distribution by geographic area for 1993, 1992 and 1991 are as follows (dollars in millions):

Year Ended December 31,	1993	1992	1991
Capital expenditures	$ 800	$ 1,083	$ 792
United States	23%	22%	25%
Africa	1%	1%	1%
European Community	33%	41%	45%
Latin America	19%	20%	14%
Northeast Europe/ Middle East	18%	13%	8%
Pacific & Canada	6%	3%	7%

In addition to capital expenditures, the Company has made significant investments in bottling operations over the last decade. The principal objective of these investments is to ensure strong and efficient production, distribution and marketing systems in order to maximize long-term growth in volume, cash flows and share-owner value of both the bottler and the Company.

When considered appropriate, the Company makes equity investments in bottling companies (typically between 20 percent and 50 percent). Through these investments, the Company is able to help focus and improve sales and marketing programs, assist in the development of effective business and information systems and help establish capital structures appropriate for these respective operations. In 1993, the Company purchased a 30 percent interest in Coca-Cola FEMSA, S.A. de C.V. (Coca-Cola FEMSA) to assist in further strengthening important bottling territories in Mexico. Also in 1993, the Company purchased shares which constitute a 10 percent voting interest in Panamerican Beverages, Inc., which owns operations in Mexico, Brazil and Colombia.

In certain situations, management believes it is advantageous to own a controlling interest in bottling operations. In 1989, the Company purchased the largest of the Coca-Cola bottling operations in France to improve the distribution system and customer relationships in that country. To compensate for limited local resources in eastern Germany, the Company invested directly in a wholly owned bottling subsidiary that could quickly capitalize on soft drink opportunities.

In restructuring the bottling system, the Company periodically takes temporary majority ownership positions in bottlers. The length of ownership is influenced by various

THE COCA-COLA COMPANY AND SUBSIDIARIES

FINANCIAL REVIEW INCORPORATING
MANAGEMENT'S DISCUSSION AND ANALYSIS

factors, including operational changes, management changes and the process of identifying appropriate new investors.

At December 31, 1993, the Company owned approximately 51 percent of Coca-Cola Amatil Limited, an Australian-based bottler of Company products. The Company intends to reduce its ownership interest to below 50 percent within the next year. Accordingly, the investment has been accounted for by the equity method of accounting.

At December 31, 1993, the Company had $69 million of investments that represented majority interests in companies other than Coca-Cola Amatil that were not consolidated. These investments were accounted for by the cost or equity methods, depending on the circumstances. These investments relate primarily to temporary majority interests that management expects to reduce to below 50 percent. For example, the Company recently reduced its voting and economic ownership interest in The Coca-Cola Bottling Company of New York, Inc. to below 50 percent, consistent with its stated intention of ending temporary control after completing certain organizational changes. Based on management's estimates, the aggregate fair values of these majority-owned investments exceeded their carrying values at December 31, 1993.

In 1993, the Company's consolidated bottling, canning and fountain/post-mix operations produced and distributed approximately 16 percent of worldwide unit case volume. Equity investee bottlers produced and distributed an additional 38 percent of worldwide unit case volume.

The following table illustrates the excess of the calculated fair values, based on quoted closing prices of publicly traded shares, for selected bottling investments over the Company's carrying values (in millions):

December 31,	Carrying Value	Fair Value	Excess
1993			
Coca-Cola Amatil Limited	$ 592	$ 1,202	$ 610
Coca-Cola Enterprises Inc.	498	859	361
Coca-Cola FEMSA, S.A. de C.V.	206	467	261
Coca-Cola Beverages Ltd.	18	98	80
Coca-Cola Bottling Co. Consolidated	86	101	15
Equity Method Investees	$ 1,400	$ 2,727	$ 1,327
Selected Cost Method Investees			
Grupo Continental, S.A.	$ 3	$ 84	$ 81
Panamerican Beverages, Inc.	32	112	80

Increasing Returns

The Company manages its concentrate and bottling operations to increase volume and its share of soft drink sales, while at the same time optimizing profit margins. The Company also provides expertise and resources to its equity investees to strengthen their businesses and to build long-term volume, cash flows and share-owner value.

Through cost control, efficient allocation of marketing resources and price increases generally in line with local inflation, the Company was able to maintain or improve margins in 1993 despite difficult economic climates in many international markets.

Increases in per capita consumption of soft drinks in the industry and the Company's share of industry sales drive the success of the Company's investments. In emerging markets, the Company's primary emphasis is raising the per capita consumption levels by expanding availability of the Company's products. In these emerging markets, investments are made in the basic infrastructure of the system: facilities, distribution networks and sales equipment. These investments are made primarily through local bottlers, matching their local expertise with the Company's focus and experience. Point-of-sale merchandising and product sampling are used to establish consumer awareness, building product acceptability. As demand expands, the Company increases consumer awareness of its products to improve the Company's share of industry sales. Advertising is used to expand the consumer's perception of appropriate consumption occasions. New products and larger packages provide the consumer with a wider array of choices.

Growth in volume and the Company's share of industry sales also depend, in part, on continuous reinvestment in advertising. Advertising establishes and builds affinity for the Company's trademarks in the minds of the consumers. Advertising expenditures were $1.1 billion in 1993 and 1992 and $1.0 billion in 1991.

Volume and profits have benefited from the Company's ownership of and investments in bottling operations. While the bottling business has relatively lower margins on revenue compared to the concentrate business, aggressive investment in soft drink infrastructure has resulted in growth in profits, share of sales and unit case volume at the bottler level, which in turn generates gallon shipment gains for the concentrate business.

**FINANCIAL REVIEW INCORPORATING
MANAGEMENT'S DISCUSSION AND ANALYSIS**

Equity income, which primarily represents returns from the Company's unconsolidated bottling investments, was $91 million in 1993. The Company's joint ventures and investments in bottling entities include Coca-Cola Enterprises Inc., Coca-Cola Amatil, Coca-Cola FEMSA and Coca-Cola & Schweppes Beverages Ltd.

Financial Policies

Maximizing share-owner value necessitates optimizing the Company's cost of capital through appropriate financial policies.

Debt Financing

The Company maintains debt levels considered prudent based on the Company's cash flows, interest coverage and the percentage of debt to the Company's total capital. The Company's overall cost of capital is lowered by the use of debt financing, resulting in increased return to share owners.

The Company's capital structure and financial policies have resulted in long-term credit ratings of "AA" from Standard & Poor's and "Aa3" from Moody's, as well as the highest credit ratings available for its commercial paper programs. The Company's strong financial position and cash flows allow for opportunistic access to financing in financial markets around the world.

Foreign Currency Management

With approximately 79 percent of operating income in 1993 generated by operations outside the United States, foreign currency management is a key element of the Company's financial policies. The Company benefits from operating in a number of different currencies, because weakness in any particular currency is often offset by strengths in other currencies. The Company closely monitors its exposure to fluctuations in currencies and, where cost-justified, adopts strategies to reduce the impact of these fluctuations on the Company's financial performance. These strategies include engaging in various hedging activities to manage income and cash flows denominated in foreign currencies, and using foreign currency borrowings when appropriate to finance investments outside the United States.

Share Repurchases

In July 1992, the Board of Directors authorized a plan to repurchase up to 100 million additional shares of the Company's common stock through the year 2000. In 1993, the Company repurchased 13 million shares approved under this plan and approximately 1 million additional shares to complete its 1989 share repurchase plan of 80 million shares. The total cost of these 1993 repurchases was approximately $586 million. From the inception of share repurchase programs in 1984 to December 31, 1993, the Company has repurchased 429 million shares at a total cost of approximately $5.8 billion. This represents over 26 percent of the Company's common shares that were outstanding at the beginning of 1984. In 1993, the Company purchased an additional 3 million shares of common stock for treasury related to the exercise of stock options by employees.

Dividend Policy

Strong earnings growth has enabled the Company to increase the cash dividend per common share by an average annual compound growth rate of 12 percent since December 31, 1983. The annual common stock dividend was $.68 per share, $.56 per share and $.48 per share in 1993, 1992 and 1991, respectively. At its February 1994 meeting, the Board of Directors increased the quarterly dividend per common share to $.195, equivalent to a full-year common dividend of $.78 in 1994. This is the 32nd consecutive year in which the Board of Directors has approved common stock dividend increases.

With approval from the Board of Directors, management has maintained a common stock dividend payout ratio of approximately 40 percent of net income. The 1993 dividend payout ratio was 41 percent.

Measuring Performance

A significant portion of the increase in the rate of growth of the Company's earnings, returns and cash flows can be attributed to the Company's actions to increase its investments in the high-margin, high-return soft drink business; increase share of sales and volume growth for its products; and manage its existing asset base effectively and efficiently.

THE COCA-COLA COMPANY AND SUBSIDIARIES

FINANCIAL REVIEW INCORPORATING MANAGEMENT'S DISCUSSION AND ANALYSIS

Economic Profit and Economic Value Added provide management a framework to measure the impact of value-oriented actions. Economic Profit is defined as net operating profit after taxes in excess of a computed capital charge for average operating capital employed. Economic Value Added represents the growth in Economic Profit from year to year.

Over the last 10 years, Economic Profit has increased at an average annual compound rate of 27 percent, resulting in Economic Value Added to the Company of $1.4 billion. Over the same period, the Company's stock price has increased at an average rate of 26 percent. Management believes that, over the long term, growth in Economic Profit, or Economic Value Added, will have a positive impact on the growth in share-owner value.

Total Return to Share Owners

During the past decade, share owners of the Company have enjoyed an excellent return on their investment. A $100 investment in the Company's common stock at December 31, 1983, together with reinvested dividends, would be worth approximately $1,286 at December 31, 1993, an average annual compound return of 29 percent.

Economic Profit and Company Stock Price

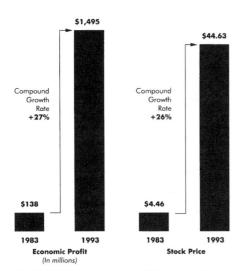

Over the last 10 years, economic profit has increased at an average rate of 27 percent, while the Company's stock has increased on average 26 percent.

MANAGEMENT'S DISCUSSION AND ANALYSIS

Lines of Business

Soft Drinks

The Company is the largest manufacturer, marketer and distributor of soft drink concentrates and syrups in the world. It manufactures soft drink concentrates and syrups, which it sells to bottling and canning operations, and manufactures fountain/post-mix soft drink syrups, which it sells to authorized fountain wholesalers and some fountain retailers. The Company has substantial equity investments in numerous soft drink bottling and canning operations, and it owns and operates certain bottling and canning operations outside the United States.

Foods

The foods business sector's principal business is processing and marketing juice and juice-drink products. It is the largest marketer of juice and juice-drink products in both the United States and the world.

Volume

Soft Drinks

The Company measures soft drink volume in two ways: gallon shipments of concentrates and syrups, and equivalent unit cases of finished product. Gallon shipments represent the primary business of the Company since they measure concentrates and syrups sold by the Company to its bottling system. Most of the Company's revenues are based on this measure of wholesale activity. The Company also monitors unit case volume, a measure of finished product sold by the bottling system to retail customers, who make sales to consumers. Management believes unit case volume more accurately measures the underlying strength of the global business system because it measures trends at the retail level and is less impacted by inventory management practices at the wholesale level. Fountain/post-mix syrups sold by the Company directly to customers are included in both measures simultaneously.

For the years 1993 and 1992, the Company increased unit case and gallon volume in its worldwide markets. The percentage increases over the prior year by geographic group and in total are as follows:

THE COCA-COLA COMPANY AND SUBSIDIARIES

FINANCIAL REVIEW INCORPORATING MANAGEMENT'S DISCUSSION AND ANALYSIS

Year Ended December 31,	1993		1992	
	Unit Cases	Gallons	Unit Cases	Gallons
Worldwide	**5%**	**4%**	3%	3%
International Sector	**6%**	**5%**	4%	3%
Africa	**4%**	**6%**	7%	10%
European Community	**1%**	**2%**	5%	3%
Latin America	**6%**	**6%**	0%	0%
Northeast Europe/ Middle East	**19%**	**20%**	21%	22%
Pacific	**7%**	**3%**	3%	2%
North America Sector[1]	**5%**	**2%**	2%	1%
United States	**5%**	**2%**	2%	2%

[1]Consists of United States and Canada.

Worldwide soft drink unit case volume increased 5 percent in 1993 as the Company expanded into new markets in East Central Europe, the Middle East and the Pacific. Volume increases in these new markets more than offset weaker than expected results in the more established markets of Europe and Japan, which suffered from record-setting cold and rainy summer seasons as well as weak economic environments. Each region experienced a volume increase over 1992 results, which were also negatively impacted by difficult economic environments in a number of the Company's major markets, including the United States and Brazil.

In 1993, unit case growth in the newly created Africa group was led by a 12 percent increase in Nigeria, resulting from increased product availability and promotions.

A cool and wet summer season slowed unit case growth in the European Community in 1993. Volume in Great Britain increased 6 percent in 1993 after growing only 3 percent in 1992.

Volume in Latin America recovered in 1993, with Mexico reporting unit case growth of 8 percent. Volume in 1992 was even with the prior year primarily because of an 18 percent decrease in unit cases in Brazil, where severe economic conditions eroded consumer purchasing power. This decline was offset by unit case volume growth of 3 percent in Mexico and 30 percent in Argentina in 1992.

Volume growth in Northeast Europe and the Middle East was driven by expansion into new markets in Poland, Romania and the remaining countries of East Central Europe and continued expansion of the Company's infrastructure in many existing markets.

In the Pacific, unit case growth in 1993 was driven by a 38 percent increase in China and a 22 percent increase in Australia. Unit case volume in Japan for 1993 was even with the prior year, reflecting the cold and wet summer. In 1992, unit cases increased 2 percent in Japan and 29 percent in China, offsetting a 1 percent decrease in the Philippines, where natural disasters hampered distribution.

In the United States, growth in the Company's fountain business drove unit case volume growth of 5 percent in 1993. Slow economic recovery impacted volume in 1992.

Foods

Year Ended December 31,	1993	1992
Total Volume	**16%**	0 %
Orange Juice	**18%**	(7)%
Other Juice Drinks	**14%**	5 %

Total unit volume in the foods business sector increased by 16 percent in 1993, driven by aggressive pricing and marketing. Total unit volume in the foods business sector was unchanged in 1992 following a 12 percent increase in volume in the prior year.

Operations
Net Operating Revenues and Gross Margin
In 1993, revenues for the Company's soft drink business increased 7 percent, reflecting an increase in gallon shipments and continued expansion of bottling and canning operations, partially offset by the adverse effect of a stronger U.S. dollar versus most key foreign currencies. Revenues for the foods business sector increased 5 percent in 1993, as volume increases more than offset price reductions.

For the Company's soft drink business, revenues grew 15 percent in 1992, primarily due to gallon shipment increases, favorable exchange movement, price increases and continued expansion of bottling and canning operations. Revenues for the foods business sector in 1992 increased 2 percent primarily due to price increases.

On a consolidated basis, the Company's worldwide net revenues grew 7 percent in 1993 while gross profit grew 10 percent. The Company's gross margin expanded to 63 percent in 1993 from 61 percent in 1992 due to lower costs for aspartame and orange solids. Gross profits grew 16 percent in 1992 on consolidated revenue growth of 13 percent.

THE COCA-COLA COMPANY AND SUBSIDIARIES

FINANCIAL REVIEW INCORPORATING MANAGEMENT'S DISCUSSION AND ANALYSIS

Selling, Administrative and General Expenses

Selling expenses were $4.4 billion in 1993, $4.0 billion in 1992 and $3.5 billion in 1991. The increase in 1993 was due primarily to increased promotional activity. The increase in 1992 was due primarily to higher marketing investments in line with expansion of the business.

Administrative and general expenses were $1.3 billion in 1993, $1.2 billion in 1992 and $1.1 billion in 1991. The increases for both years were due primarily to expansion of the business, particularly newly formed, Company-owned bottling operations. Also, administrative and general expenses in 1993 include provisions of $63 million related to increasing efficiencies in European, domestic and corporate operations. Administrative and general expenses, as a percentage of net operating revenues, were approximately 10 percent in 1993 and 1992 and 9 percent in 1991.

Operating Income and Operating Margin

Operating income grew 12 percent in 1993, after increasing 19 percent in 1992. Operating margins grew to 22 percent in 1993 from 21 percent in 1992. The expansion in operating margins resulted from gross margin expansion.

Margin Analysis

■ **Net Operating Revenues** *(In billions)*
■ **Gross Margin**
■ **Operating Margin**

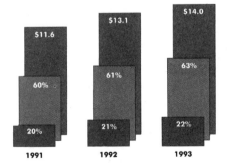

$11.6	$13.1	$14.0
60%	61%	63%
20%	21%	22%
1991	1992	1993

The Company's gross profit and operating income have increased due to both growth in revenues and expansion of margins.

Interest Income and Interest Expense

In 1993, interest expense was approximately even with the prior year while interest income decreased 12 percent. Interest income and interest expense declined in 1992, primarily due to lower interest rates.

Equity Income

Equity income increased 40 percent in 1993 due primarily to new bottling investments and improved results at Coca-Cola Amatil and Coca-Cola Nestlé Refreshments, offset by the results at the Company's Canadian affiliate, Coca-Cola Beverages Ltd. In the fourth quarter, Coca-Cola Beverages recorded a pretax restructuring charge of $126 million, which reduced the Company's equity income by $42 million.

Equity income increased 63 percent, to $65 million, in 1992 due primarily to one-time charges recorded by Coca-Cola Enterprises in 1991, partially offset by increased start-up costs of Coca-Cola Nestlé Refreshments in 1992.

Other Income (Deductions)-Net

In 1993, other income (deductions)-net increased $86 million, primarily due to gains on sales of certain real estate and bottling investments. This includes a $50 million pretax gain recognized on the sale of citrus groves in the United States and a $34 million pretax gain recognized on the sale of property no longer required as a result of a consolidation of manufacturing operations in Japan.

Other income (deductions)-net in 1992 was lower than 1991 due to nonrecurring gains recorded in 1991.

Gain on Issuance of Stock by Coca-Cola Amatil

In the fourth quarter of 1993, Coca-Cola Amatil purchased a bottling operation in Indonesia by issuing approximately 8 million shares of common stock, which resulted in a non-cash pretax gain of $12 million for the Company.

FINANCIAL REVIEW INCORPORATING
MANAGEMENT'S DISCUSSION AND ANALYSIS

Income Taxes

The Company's effective tax rate was 31.3 percent in 1993, 31.4 percent in 1992 and 32.1 percent in 1991. The Company's effective tax rate reflects the favorable U.S. tax treatment from manufacturing facilities in Puerto Rico that operate under a negotiated exemption grant as well as the tax benefit derived from significant operations outside the United States which are taxed at rates lower than the U.S. statutory rate of 35 percent. Changes to U.S. tax law enacted in 1993 will limit the utilization of the favorable tax treatment from operations in Puerto Rico beginning in 1994, and will exert upward pressure on the Company's effective tax rate.

Transition Effect of Changes in Accounting Principles

As of January 1, 1993, the Company recognized an after-tax charge of $12 million resulting from the adoption of Statement of Financial Accounting Standards No. 112, Employers' Accounting for Postemployment Benefits (SFAS 112). The cumulative charge consists primarily of health benefits for surviving spouses and disabled employees.

As of January 1, 1992, the Company recognized an after-tax charge of $219 million resulting from the adoption of Statement of Financial Accounting Standards No. 106, Employers' Accounting for Postretirement Benefits Other Than Pensions (SFAS 106). The cumulative charge consists of postretirement health care and life insurance benefit obligations to employees of the Company and the Company's portion of postretirement benefit obligations of its equity investees. The Company elected to absorb this charge immediately rather than amortize the obligation over a period of up to 20 years.

Income Per Common Share

Accelerated by the Company's share repurchase program, income per common share before changes in accounting principles grew 17 percent and 18 percent in 1993 and 1992, respectively. Net income per common share grew 33 percent in 1993, reflecting the $.17 per share impact of the adoption of SFAS 106 in 1992.

Liquidity and Capital Resources

One of the Company's financial strengths is its ability to generate cash from operations in excess of requirements for capital reinvestment and dividends.

Free Cash Flow

Free Cash Flow is the cash from operations remaining after the Company has satisfied its business reinvestment opportunities. Management focuses on growing long-term Free Cash Flow to achieve management's primary objective, maximizing share-owner value. The Company uses Free Cash Flow, along with borrowings, to make share repurchases and dividend payments. The consolidated statements of cash flows are summarized as follows (in millions):

Year Ended December 31,	1993	1992	1991
Cash flows provided by (used in):			
Operations	$ 2,508	$ 2,232	$ 2,084
Investment activities	(885)	(1,359)	(1,124)
Free Cash Flow	1,623	873	960
Cash flows provided by (used in):			
Financing	(1,540)	(917)	(1,331)
Exchange	(41)	(58)	—
Increase (decrease) in cash	$ 42	$ (102)	$ (371)

Cash provided by operations continued to grow in 1993, reaching $2.5 billion, resulting from growth in net income before the noncash charges for depreciation and amortization. In 1992, cash from operations totaled $2.2 billion, a 7 percent increase over 1991. After extensive investment in eastern Europe and other emerging markets during 1992, the Company's purchases of property, plant and equipment declined $283 million in 1993. This decline, coupled with the receipt of proceeds on the sales of real estate in Japan and the United States and various bottling investments, resulted in a decrease in cash used in investment activities in 1993. Cash used in investment activities increased in 1992 due primarily to purchases of property, plant and equipment, investments and acquisitions of bottling operations, offset by the collection of certain finance subsidiary receivables added in 1991.

The finance subsidiary made additional borrowings in 1993 to fund increased receivables. The increase in marketable securities and other assets in 1993 and 1992 was primarily attributed to an increase in marketable securities held in accordance with a negotiated income tax exemption

**FINANCIAL REVIEW INCORPORATING
MANAGEMENT'S DISCUSSION AND ANALYSIS**

grant for the Company's manufacturing facilities in Puerto Rico. The balance also increased due to additional deferred tax assets in 1993. Timing of tax payments, including those attributable to the sales of real estate, resulted in an increase in accrued taxes of 33 percent in 1993. In 1992, payments collected by the finance subsidiary were used to reduce notes payable. The noncash charge for the change in accounting for postretirement benefits other than pensions resulted in an increase in other long-term liabilities and a decrease in deferred tax liabilities in 1992.

Financing

Financing activities primarily represent the Company's net borrowing activities, dividend payments and share repurchases. Cash used in financing activities totaled $1.5 billion in 1993, $917 million in 1992 and $1.3 billion in 1991. The change between years was due primarily to net reductions of debt in 1993 and 1991 compared to net borrowings in 1992. Cash used to purchase common stock for treasury decreased to $680 million in 1993, from $1.3 billion in 1992.

The Company aggressively manages its mix of short-term versus long-term debt to lower its overall cost of borrowing. This process, coupled with the share repurchase program and investment activity, resulted in current liabilities exceeding current assets at December 31, 1993.

The Company manages its debt levels based on the following financial measurements and ratios:

Year Ended December 31,	**1993**	1992	1991
Net debt (in billions)	**$1.6**	$1.8	$1.0
Net debt to net capital	**26%**	32%	19%
Free cash flow to net debt	**100%**	48%	95%
Interest coverage	**18x**	16x	13x
Ratio of earnings to fixed charges	**15.7x**	14.1x	11.6x

Debt levels are measured excluding the debt of the Company's finance subsidiary, and are net of cash, cash equivalents and marketable securities in excess of operating requirements and net of temporary bottling investments.

At December 31, 1993, the Company had $1.4 billion in lines of credit and other short-term credit facilities contractually available, under which $150 million was outstanding. Included were $1.0 billion in lines designated to support commercial paper and other borrowings, under which no amounts were outstanding at December 31, 1993.

Exchange

International operations are subject to certain opportunities and risks, including currency fluctuations and government actions. The Company closely monitors its methods of operating in each country and adopts strategies responsive to changing economic and political environments.

The Company uses approximately 46 functional currencies. In 1993, 1992 and 1991, weighted average exchange rates for certain key foreign currencies that are traded on exchange markets strengthened (weakened) against the U.S. dollar as follows:

Year Ended December 31,	**1993**	1992	1991
Key market-traded currencies	**(3)%**	5 %	1 %
Australian dollar	**(7)%**	(5)%	1 %
British pound	**(15)%**	1 %	(1)%
Canadian dollar	**(8)%**	(4)%	1 %
German mark	**(5)%**	8 %	(3)%
Japanese yen	**15 %**	6 %	8 %

The change in the foreign currency translation adjustment in 1993 was due primarily to the weakening of certain European currencies against the U.S. dollar. Exchange losses recorded in other income (deductions)-net amounted to $74 million in 1993, $25 million in 1992 and $22 million in 1991. Exchange losses include the remeasurement of certain currencies into functional currencies and costs of hedging certain transaction and balance sheet exposures. Additional information concerning the Company's hedging activities is presented on page 63.

Impact of Inflation and Changing Prices

Inflation is a factor in many markets around the world and consequently impacts the way the Company operates. In general, management believes the Company is able to increase prices to counteract the effects of increasing costs and generate sufficient cash flows to maintain its productive capability.

Additional Information

For additional information concerning the Company's operations, cash flows, liquidity and capital resources, this analysis should be read in conjunction with the information on pages 54 through 72 of this report. Additional information concerning operations in different lines of business and geographic areas is presented on pages 69 and 70.

THE COCA-COLA COMPANY AND SUBSIDIARIES

SELECTED FINANCIAL DATA

	Compound Growth Rates		Year Ended December 31	
(In millions except per share data, ratios and growth rates)	5 Years	10 Years	1993[2]	1992[3,4]
Summary of Operations				
Net operating revenues	11.6%	10.7%	$13,957	$13,074
Cost of goods sold	8.5%	7.2%	5,160	5,055
Gross profit	13.7%	13.5%	8,797	8,019
Selling, administrative and general expenses	13.4%	13.2%	5,695	5,249
Operating income	14.2%	14.1%	3,102	2,770
Interest income			144	164
Interest expense			168	171
Equity income			91	65
Other income (deductions)-net			4	(82)
Gain on issuance of stock by subsidiaries			12	—
Income from continuing operations before income taxes and changes in accounting principles	14.4%	13.8%	3,185	2,746
Income taxes	13.2%	10.3%	997	863
Income from continuing operations before changes in accounting principles	15.0%	15.8%	$ 2,188	$ 1,883
Net income	15.8%	14.6%	$ 2,176	$ 1,664
Preferred stock dividends			—	—
Net income available to common share owners	16.0%	14.6%	$ 2,176	$ 1,664
Average common shares outstanding			1,302	1,317
Per Common Share Data				
Income from continuing operations before changes in accounting principles	17.8%	18.4%	$ 1.68	$ 1.43
Net income	18.7%	17.3%	1.67	1.26
Cash dividends	17.8%	11.9%	.68	.56
Market price at December 31	31.9%	25.9%	44.63	41.88
Balance Sheet Data				
Cash, cash equivalents and current marketable securities			$ 1,078	$ 1,063
Property, plant and equipment—net			3,729	3,526
Depreciation			333	310
Capital expenditures			800	1,083
Total assets			12,021	11,052
Long-term debt			1,428	1,120
Total debt			3,100	3,207
Share-owners' equity			4,584	3,888
Total capital[1]			7,684	7,095
Other Key Financial Measures[1]				
Total-debt-to-total-capital			40.3%	45.2%
Net-debt-to-net-capital			26.2%	31.9%
Return on common equity			51.7%	46.4%
Return on capital			31.2%	29.4%
Dividend payout ratio			40.6%	44.3%
Economic profit			$ 1,495	$ 1,293

[1] See Glossary on page 76.
[2] In 1993, the Company adopted SFAS No. 112, Employers' Accounting for Postemployment Benefits.
[3] In 1992, the Company adopted SFAS No. 106, Employers' Accounting for Postretirement Benefits Other Than Pensions.
[4] The Company adopted SFAS No. 109, Accounting for Income Taxes, in 1992 by restating financial statements beginning in 1989.

THE COCA-COLA COMPANY AND SUBSIDIARIES

1991[4]	1990[4]	1989[4]	1988	1987	1986	1985	1984	1983
$11,572	$10,236	$8,622	$8,065	$7,658	$6,977	$5,879	$5,442	$5,056
4,649	4,208	3,548	3,429	3,633	3,454	2,909	2,738	2,580
6,923	6,028	5,074	4,636	4,025	3,523	2,970	2,704	2,476
4,604	4,076	3,348	3,038	2,701	2,626	2,163	1,855	1,648
2,319	1,952	1,726	1,598	1,324	897	807	849	828
175	170	205	199	232	154	151	133	90
192	231	308	230	297	208	196	128	77
40	110	75	92	64	45	52	42	35
41	13	66	(33)	—	35	69	13	2
—	—	—	—	40	375	—	—	—
2,383	2,014	1,764	1,626	1,363	1,298	883	909	878
765	632	553	537	496	471	314	360	374
$ 1,618	$ 1,382	$1,211	$1,089	$ 867	$ 827	$ 569	$ 549	$ 504
$ 1,618	$ 1,382	$1,537	$1,045	$ 916	$ 934	$ 722	$ 629	$ 559
1	18	21	7	—	—	—	—	—
$ 1,617	$ 1,364	$1,516[5]	$1,038	$ 916	$ 934	$ 722	$ 629	$ 559
1,333	1,337	1,384	1,458	1,509	1,547	1,573	1,587	1,635
$ 1.21	$ 1.02	$ .86	$ .74	$ .57	$ .53	$ .36	$ .35	$ .31
1.21	1.02	1.10[5]	.71	.61	.60	.46	.40	.34
.48	.40	.34	.30	.28	.26	.25	.23	.22
40.13	23.25	19.31	11.16	9.53	9.44	7.04	5.20	4.46
$ 1,117	$ 1,492	$1,182	$1,231	$1,489	$ 895	$ 843	$ 768	$ 559
2,890	2,386	2,021	1,759	1,602	1,538	1,483	1,284	1,247
254	236	181	167	152	151	130	119	111
792	593	462	387	304	346	412	300	324
10,189	9,245	8,249	7,451	8,606	7,675	6,341	5,241	4,540
985	536	549	761	909	996	801	631	428
2,288	2,537	1,980	2,124	2,995	1,848	1,280	1,310	520
4,239	3,662	3,299	3,345	3,187	3,479	2,948	2,751	2,912
6,527	6,199	5,279	5,469	6,182	5,327	4,228	4,061	3,432
35.1%	40.9%	37.5%	38.8%	48.4%	34.7%	30.3%	32.3%	15.2%
19.2%	23.7%	14.7%	18.9%	15.4%	10.9%	15.6%	19.7%	5.6%
41.3%	41.4%	39.4%	34.7%	26.0%	25.7%	20.0%	19.4%	17.7%
27.5%	26.8%	26.5%	21.3%	18.3%	20.1%	16.8%	16.7%	16.4%
39.5%	39.2%	31.0%[5]	42.1%	46.0%	43.1%	53.8%	57.9%	65.3%
$ 1,029	$ 878	$ 821	$ 748	$ 417	$ 311	$ 269	$ 268	$ 138

[5]Net income available to common share owners in 1989 includes after-tax gains of $604 million ($.44 per common share) from the sales of the Company's equity interest in Columbia Pictures Entertainment, Inc. and the Company's bottled water business and the transition effect of $265 million related to the change in accounting for income taxes. Excluding these nonrecurring items, the dividend payout ratio in 1989 was 39.9 percent.

THE COCA-COLA COMPANY AND SUBSIDIARIES

CONSOLIDATED BALANCE SHEETS

December 31,	1993	1992
(In millions except share data)		
Assets		
Current		
Cash and cash equivalents	$ 998	$ 956
Marketable securities, at cost	80	107
	1,078	1,063
Trade accounts receivable, less allowances of $39 in 1993 and $33 in 1992	1,210	1,055
Finance subsidiary receivables	33	31
Inventories	1,049	1,019
Prepaid expenses and other assets	1,064	1,080
Total Current Assets	4,434	4,248
Investments and Other Assets		
Investments		
Coca-Cola Enterprises Inc.	498	518
Coca-Cola Amatil Limited	592	548
Other, principally bottling companies	1,125	1,097
Finance subsidiary receivables	226	95
Marketable securities and other assets	868	637
	3,309	2,895
Property, Plant and Equipment		
Land	197	203
Buildings and improvements	1,616	1,529
Machinery and equipment	3,380	3,137
Containers	403	374
	5,596	5,243
Less allowances for depreciation	1,867	1,717
	3,729	3,526
Goodwill and Other Intangible Assets	549	383
	$ 12,021	$ 11,052

THE COCA-COLA COMPANY AND SUBSIDIARIES

December 31,	1993	1992
Liabilities and Share-Owners' Equity		
Current		
Accounts payable and accrued expenses	**$ 2,217**	$ 2,253
Loans and notes payable	**1,409**	1,967
Finance subsidiary notes payable	**244**	105
Current maturities of long-term debt	**19**	15
Accrued taxes	**1,282**	963
Total Current Liabilities	**5,171**	5,303
Long-Term Debt	**1,428**	1,120
Other Liabilities	**725**	659
Deferred Income Taxes	**113**	82
Share-Owners' Equity		
Common stock, $.25 par value—		
Authorized: 2,800,000,000 shares		
Issued: 1,703,526,299 shares in 1993; 1,696,202,840 shares in 1992	**426**	424
Capital surplus	**1,086**	871
Reinvested earnings	**9,458**	8,165
Unearned compensation related to outstanding restricted stock	**(85)**	(100)
Foreign currency translation adjustment	**(420)**	(271)
	10,465	9,089
Less treasury stock, at cost (406,072,817 common shares in 1993; 389,431,622 common shares in 1992)	**5,881**	5,201
	4,584	3,888
	$ 12,021	$ 11,052

See Notes to Consolidated Financial Statements.

THE COCA-COLA COMPANY AND SUBSIDIARIES

CONSOLIDATED STATEMENTS OF INCOME

Year Ended December 31, (In millions except per share data)	1993	1992	1991
Net Operating Revenues	**$ 13,957**	$ 13,074	$ 11,572
Cost of goods sold	**5,160**	5,055	4,649
Gross Profit	**8,797**	8,019	6,923
Selling, administrative and general expenses	**5,695**	5,249	4,604
Operating Income	**3,102**	2,770	2,319
Interest income	**144**	164	175
Interest expense	**168**	171	192
Equity income	**91**	65	40
Other income (deductions)-net	**4**	(82)	41
Gain on issuance of stock by Coca-Cola Amatil	**12**	—	—
Income before Income Taxes and Changes in Accounting Principles	**3,185**	2,746	2,383
Income taxes	**997**	863	765
Income before Changes in Accounting Principles	**2,188**	1,883	1,618
Transition effects of changes in accounting principles			
Postemployment benefits	**(12)**	—	—
Postretirement benefits other than pensions			
Consolidated operations	**—**	(146)	—
Equity investments	**—**	(73)	—
Net Income	**2,176**	1,664	1,618
Preferred stock dividends	**—**	—	1
Net Income Available to Common Share Owners	**$ 2,176**	$ 1,664	$ 1,617
Income per Common Share			
Before changes in accounting principles	**$ 1.68**	$ 1.43	$ 1.21
Transition effects of changes in accounting principles			
Postemployment benefits	**(.01)**	—	—
Postretirement benefits other than pensions			
Consolidated operations	**—**	(.11)	—
Equity investments	**—**	(.06)	—
Net Income per Common Share	**$ 1.67**	$ 1.26	$ 1.21
Average Common Shares Outstanding	**1,302**	1,317	1,333

See Notes to Consolidated Financial Statements.

THE COCA-COLA COMPANY AND SUBSIDIARIES

CONSOLIDATED STATEMENTS OF CASH FLOWS

Year Ended December 31,	1993	1992	1991
(In millions)			
Operating Activities			
Net income	$ 2,176	$ 1,664	$ 1,618
Transition effects of changes in accounting principles	12	219	—
Depreciation and amortization	360	322	261
Deferred income taxes	(62)	(27)	(94)
Equity income, net of dividends	(35)	(30)	(16)
Foreign currency adjustments	9	24	66
Gains on sales of assets	(84)	—	(35)
Other noncash items	78	103	33
Net change in operating assets and liabilities	54	(43)	251
Net cash provided by operating activities	2,508	2,232	2,084
Investing Activities			
Decrease (increase) in current marketable securities	29	(52)	3
Additions to finance subsidiary receivables	(177)	(54)	(210)
Collections of finance subsidiary receivables	44	254	52
Acquisitions and purchases of investments	(816)	(717)	(399)
Proceeds from disposals of investments and other assets	621	247	180
Purchases of property, plant and equipment	(800)	(1,083)	(792)
Proceeds from disposals of property, plant and equipment	312	47	44
All other investing activities	(98)	(1)	(2)
Net cash used in investing activities	(885)	(1,359)	(1,124)
Net cash provided by operations after reinvestment	1,623	873	960
Financing Activities			
Issuances of debt	445	1,381	990
Payments of debt	(567)	(432)	(1,246)
Preferred stock redeemed	—	—	(75)
Common stock issued	145	131	39
Purchases of common stock for treasury	(680)	(1,259)	(399)
Dividends (common and preferred)	(883)	(738)	(640)
Net cash used in financing activities	(1,540)	(917)	(1,331)
Effect of Exchange Rate Changes on Cash and Cash Equivalents	(41)	(58)	—
Cash and Cash Equivalents			
Net increase (decrease) during the year	42	(102)	(371)
Balance at beginning of year	956	1,058	1,429
Balance at end of year	$ 998	$ 956	$ 1,058

See Notes to Consolidated Financial Statements.

THE COCA-COLA COMPANY AND SUBSIDIARIES

CONSOLIDATED STATEMENTS OF SHARE-OWNERS' EQUITY

Three Years Ended December 31, 1993	Preferred Stock	Common Stock	Capital Surplus	Reinvested Earnings	Outstanding Restricted Stock	Foreign Currency Translation	Treasury Stock
(In millions except per share data)							
Balance December 31, 1990	$ 75	$ 420	$ 513	$ 6,261	$ (68)	$ 4	$ (3,543)
Sales of stock to employees exercising stock options	—	1	38	—	—	—	(2)
Tax benefit from employees' stock option and restricted stock plans	—	—	20	—	—	—	—
Translation adjustments	—	—	—	—	—	(9)	—
Stock issued under restricted stock plans, less amortization of $22	—	1	69	—	(47)	—	—
Purchases of common stock for treasury	—	—	—	—	—	—	(397)
Redemption of preferred stock	(75)	—	—	—	—	—	—
Net income	—	—	—	1,618	—	—	—
Dividends							
Preferred	—	—	—	(1)	—	—	—
Common (per share–$.48)	—	—	—	(639)	—	—	—
Balance December 31, 1991	—	422	640	7,239	(115)	(5)	(3,942)
Sales of stock to employees exercising stock options	—	2	129	—	—	—	(34)
Tax benefit from employees' stock option and restricted stock plans	—	—	93	—	—	—	—
Translation adjustments	—	—	—	—	—	(266)	—
Stock issued under restricted stock plans, less amortization of $25	—	—	9	—	15	—	—
Purchases of common stock for treasury	—	—	—	—	—	—	(1,225)
Net income	—	—	—	1,664	—	—	—
Common dividends (per share–$.56)	—	—	—	(738)	—	—	—
Balance December 31, 1992	—	424	871	8,165	(100)	(271)	(5,201)
Sales of stock to employees exercising stock options	—	2	143	—	—	—	(94)
Tax benefit from employees' stock option and restricted stock plans	—	—	66	—	—	—	—
Translation adjustments	—	—	—	—	—	(149)	—
Stock issued under restricted stock plans, less amortization of $19	—	—	6	—	15	—	—
Purchases of common stock for treasury	—	—	—	—	—	—	(586)
Net income	—	—	—	2,176	—	—	—
Common dividends (per share–$.68)	—	—	—	(883)	—	—	—
Balance December 31, 1993	$ —	$ 426	$ 1,086	$ 9,458	$ (85)	$ (420)	$ (5,881)

See Notes to Consolidated Financial Statements.

THE COCA-COLA COMPANY AND SUBSIDIARIES

NOTES TO CONSOLIDATED FINANCIAL STATEMENTS

1. Accounting Policies

The significant accounting policies and practices followed by The Coca-Cola Company and subsidiaries (the Company) are as follows:

Consolidation

The consolidated financial statements include the accounts of the Company and all subsidiaries except where control is temporary or does not rest with the Company. The Company's investments in companies in which it has the ability to exercise significant influence over operating and financial policies, including certain investments where there is a temporary majority interest, are accounted for by the equity method. Accordingly, the Company's share of the net earnings of these companies is included in consolidated net income. The Company's investments in other companies are carried at cost. All significant intercompany accounts and transactions are eliminated.

Certain amounts in the prior years' financial statements have been reclassified to conform to the current-year presentation.

Net Income per Common Share

Net income per common share is computed by dividing net income less dividends on preferred stock by the weighted average number of common shares outstanding.

Cash Equivalents

Marketable securities that are highly liquid and have maturities of three months or less at the date of purchase are classified as cash equivalents.

Inventories

Inventories are valued at the lower of cost or market. In general, cost is determined on the basis of average cost or first-in, first-out methods. However, for certain inventories, cost is determined on the last-in, first-out (LIFO) method. The excess of current costs over LIFO stated values amounted to approximately $9 million and $24 million at December 31, 1993 and 1992, respectively.

Property, Plant and Equipment

Property, plant and equipment are stated at cost, less allowances for depreciation. Property, plant and equipment are depreciated principally by the straight-line method over the estimated useful lives of the assets.

Goodwill and Other Intangible Assets

Goodwill and other intangible assets are stated on the basis of cost and are being amortized, principally on a straight-line basis, over the estimated future periods to be benefited (not exceeding 40 years). Accumulated amortization was approximately $50 million and $26 million at December 31, 1993 and 1992, respectively.

Changes in Accounting Principles

Statement of Financial Accounting Standards No. 112, Employers' Accounting for Postemployment Benefits (SFAS 112), was adopted as of January 1, 1993. SFAS 112 requires employers to accrue the costs of benefits to former or inactive employees after employment, but before retirement. The Company recorded an accumulated obligation of $12 million, which is net of deferred taxes of $8 million. The increase in annual pretax postemployment benefits expense in 1993 was immaterial to Company operations.

In 1993, the Financial Accounting Standards Board (FASB) issued Statement of Financial Accounting Standards No. 115, Accounting for Certain Investments in Debt and Equity Securities (SFAS 115). SFAS 115 requires that the carrying value of certain investments be adjusted to their fair value. The Company's required adoption date is January 1, 1994. The Company expects to record an increase to share-owners' equity of approximately $65 million in 1994 from the adoption of SFAS 115.

2. Inventories

Inventories consist of the following (in millions):

December 31,	1993	1992
Raw materials and supplies	$ 689	$ 620
Work in process	4	23
Finished goods	356	376
	$1,049	$1,019

3. Bottling Investments

The Company invests in bottling companies to ensure the strongest and most efficient production, distribution and marketing systems possible.

Coca-Cola Enterprises Inc.

Coca-Cola Enterprises is the largest bottler of Company products in the world. The Company owns approximately 44 percent of the outstanding common stock of Coca-Cola Enterprises, and, accordingly, accounts for its investment by the equity method of accounting. A summary of financial information for Coca-Cola Enterprises is as follows (in millions):

THE COCA-COLA COMPANY AND SUBSIDIARIES

NOTES TO CONSOLIDATED FINANCIAL STATEMENTS

December 31,	1993	1992
Current assets	$ 746	$ 701
Noncurrent assets	7,936	7,384
Total assets	$8,682	$8,085
Current liabilities	$1,007	$1,304
Noncurrent liabilities	6,415	5,527
Total liabilities	$7,422	$6,831
Share-owners' equity	$1,260	$1,254
Company equity investment	$ 498	$ 518

Year Ended December 31,	1993	1992	1991
Net operating revenues	$5,465	$ 5,127	$3,915
Cost of goods sold	3,372	3,219	2,420
Gross profit	$2,093	$ 1,908	$1,495
Operating income	$ 385	$ 306	$ 120
Operating cash flow[1]	$ 804	$ 695	$ 538
Loss before changes in accounting principles	$ (15)	$ (15)	$ (83)
Net loss available to common share owners	$ (15)	$ (186)	$ (92)
Company equity loss	$ (6)	$ (6)	$ (40)

[1]Excludes nonrecurring charges.

The above 1992 net loss of Coca-Cola Enterprises includes $171 million of noncash, after-tax charges resulting from the adoption of Statement of Financial Accounting Standards No. 106, Employers' Accounting for Post-retirement Benefits Other Than Pensions (SFAS 106) and Statement of Financial Accounting Standards No. 109, Accounting for Income Taxes (SFAS 109) as of January 1, 1992. The Company's financial statements reflect the adoption of SFAS 109 by Coca-Cola Enterprises as if it occurred on January 1, 1989.

The 1991 results of Coca-Cola Enterprises include pretax restructuring charges of $152 million and a pretax charge of $15 million to increase insurance reserves.

In a 1991 merger, Coca-Cola Enterprises acquired Johnston Coca-Cola Bottling Group, Inc. (Johnston) for approximately $196 million in cash and 13 million shares of Coca-Cola Enterprises common stock. The Company exchanged its 22 percent ownership interest in Johnston for approximately $81 million in cash and approximately 50,000 shares of Coca-Cola Enterprises common stock, resulting in a pretax gain of $27 million to the Company. The Company's ownership interest in Coca-Cola Enterprises was reduced from 49 percent to approximately 44 percent as a result of this transaction.

If the Johnston acquisition had been completed on January 1, 1991, Coca-Cola Enterprises' 1991 pro forma net loss available to common share owners would have been approximately $137 million. Summarized financial information and net concentrate/syrup sales related to Johnston prior to its acquisition by Coca-Cola Enterprises have been combined with other equity investments below.

Net concentrate/syrup sales to Coca-Cola Enterprises were $961 million in 1993, $889 million in 1992 and $626 million in 1991. Coca-Cola Enterprises purchases sweeteners through the Company under a pass-through arrangement, and, accordingly, related collections from Coca-Cola Enterprises and payments to suppliers are not included in the Company's consolidated statements of income. These transactions amounted to $211 million in 1993, $225 million in 1992 and $185 million in 1991. The Company also provides certain administrative and other services to Coca-Cola Enterprises under negotiated fee arrangements.

The Company engages in a wide range of marketing programs, media advertising and other similar arrangements to promote the sale of Company products in territories in which Coca-Cola Enterprises operates. The Company's direct support for certain Coca-Cola Enterprises' marketing activities and participation with Coca-Cola Enterprises in cooperative advertising and other marketing programs amounted to approximately $256 million in 1993, $253 million in 1992 and $199 million in 1991.

In April 1993, the Company purchased majority ownership interests in two bottling companies in Tennessee along with the rights to purchase the remaining minority interests. Such ownership interests and a bottling operation in the Netherlands were sold to Coca-Cola Enterprises in June 1993. The Company received approximately $260 million in cash plus the assumption of indebtedness and carrying costs resulting in an after-tax gain of $11 million or approximately $.01 per share.

In 1992, the Company sold 100 percent of the common stock of the Erie, Pennsylvania, Coca-Cola bottler to Coca-Cola Enterprises for approximately $11 million, which approximated the Company's original investment plus carrying costs. In January 1994, the Company sold common stock representing a 9 percent voting interest in The Coca-Cola Bottling Company of New York, Inc. (CCNY) to Coca-Cola Enterprises for approximately $6 million, which approximated the Company's investment.

THE COCA-COLA COMPANY AND SUBSIDIARIES

NOTES TO CONSOLIDATED FINANCIAL STATEMENTS

If valued at the December 31, 1993, quoted closing price of the publicly traded Coca-Cola Enterprises shares, the calculated value of the Company's investment in Coca-Cola Enterprises would have exceeded its carrying value by approximately $361 million.

Other Equity Investments

The Company owns approximately 51 percent of Coca-Cola Amatil, an Australian-based bottler of Company products. In the fourth quarter of 1993, Coca-Cola Amatil issued approximately 8 million shares of stock to acquire the Company's franchise bottler in Jakarta, Indonesia. This transaction resulted in a pretax gain of approximately $12 million and diluted the Company's ownership interest to the present level. The Company intends to reduce its ownership interest in Coca-Cola Amatil to below 50 percent. Accordingly, the investment has been accounted for by the equity method of accounting.

At December 31, 1993, the excess of the Company's investment over its equity in the underlying net assets of Coca-Cola Amatil was approximately $191 million, which is being amortized over 40 years. The Company recorded equity income from Coca-Cola Amatil of $40 million, $28 million and $15 million in 1993, 1992 and 1991, respectively. These amounts are net of the amortization charges discussed above.

In January 1993, Coca-Cola Amatil sold its snack-food segment for approximately $299 million, and recognized a gain of $169 million. The Company's ownership interest in the sale proceeds received by Coca-Cola Amatil approximated the carrying value of the Company's investment in the snack-food segment.

In 1993, the Company acquired a 30 percent equity interest in Coca-Cola FEMSA, S.A. de C.V., which operates bottling facilities in the Valley of Mexico and Mexico's southeastern region, for $195 million. At December 31, 1993, the excess of the Company's investment over its equity in the underlying net assets of Coca-Cola FEMSA was approximately $130 million, which is being amortized over 40 years.

Also in 1993, the Company entered into a joint venture with Coca-Cola Bottling Co. Consolidated (Consolidated), establishing the Piedmont Coca-Cola Bottling Partnership (Piedmont), which will operate certain bottling territories in the United States acquired from each company. The Company has made a cash contribution of $70 million to the partnership for a 50 percent ownership interest. Consolidated has contributed bottling assets valued at approximately $48 million and approximately $22 million in cash for the remaining 50 percent interest. Piedmont has purchased assets and stock of certain bottling companies from the Company for approximately $163 million, which approximated the Company's carrying cost, and certain bottling assets from Consolidated for approximately $130 million. The Company beneficially owns a 30 percent economic interest and a 23 percent voting interest in Consolidated.

Operating results include the Company's proportionate share of income from equity investments since the respective dates of investment. A summary of financial information for the Company's equity investments, other than Coca-Cola Enterprises, is as follows (in millions):

December 31,	1993	1992
Current assets	$ 2,294	$ 1,945
Noncurrent assets	4,780	4,172
Total assets	$ 7,074	$ 6,117
Current liabilities	$ 1,926	$ 2,219
Noncurrent liabilities	2,366	1,720
Total liabilities	$ 4,292	$ 3,939
Share-owners' equity	$ 2,782	$ 2,178
Company equity investments	$ 1,629	$ 1,387

Year Ended December 31,	1993	1992	1991
Net operating revenues	$ 8,168	$ 7,027	$ 7,877
Cost of goods sold	5,385	4,740	5,244
Gross profit	$ 2,783	$ 2,287	$ 2,633
Operating income	$ 673	$ 364	$ 560
Operating cash flow	$ 984	$ 923	$ 979
Income before changes in accounting principles	$ 258	$ 199	$ 214
Net income	$ 258	$ 74	$ 214
Company equity income	$ 97	$ 71	$ 80

Equity investments include certain non-bottling investees.

Net income for the Company's equity investments in 1993 reflects an $86 million after-tax charge recorded by Coca-Cola Beverages Ltd., related to restructuring its operations in Canada.

Net sales to equity investees, other than Coca-Cola Enterprises, were $1.2 billion in 1993 and $1.3 billion in 1992 and 1991. The Company participates in various marketing, promotional and other activities with these investees, the majority of which are located outside the United States.

THE COCA-COLA COMPANY AND SUBSIDIARIES

NOTES TO CONSOLIDATED FINANCIAL STATEMENTS

If valued at the December 31, 1993, quoted closing prices of shares actively traded on stock markets, the net calculated value of the Company's equity investments in publicly traded bottlers, other than Coca-Cola Enterprises, would have exceeded the Company's carrying value by approximately $966 million.

The consolidated balance sheet caption Other, principally bottling companies, also includes various investments that are accounted for by the cost method.

4. Finance Subsidiary

Coca-Cola Financial Corporation (CCFC) provides loans and other forms of financing to Coca-Cola bottlers and customers for the acquisition of sales-related equipment and for other business purposes. The approximate contractual maturities of finance receivables for the five years succeeding December 31, 1993, are as follows (in millions):

1994	1995	1996	1997	1998
$33	$32	$31	$16	$118

These amounts do not reflect possible prepayments or renewals.

In 1993, CCFC provided a $100 million subordinated loan to CCNY and issued a $50 million letter of credit on CCNY's behalf, of which $18 million was outstanding at December 31, 1993.

In connection with the 1991 acquisition of Sunbelt Coca-Cola Bottling Company, Inc. by Consolidated, CCFC purchased 25,000 shares of Consolidated preferred stock for $50 million, provided to Consolidated a $153 million bridge loan and issued a $77 million letter of credit on Consolidated's behalf. Consolidated redeemed the 25,000 shares of preferred stock for $50 million plus accrued dividends in 1992. Consolidated also repaid all amounts due under the bridge loan in 1992. In 1993, the letter of credit was withdrawn.

5. Accounts Payable and Accrued Expenses

Accounts payable and accrued expenses consist of the following (in millions):

December 31,	1993	1992
Accrued marketing	$ 371	$ 374
Container deposits	122	117
Accrued compensation	119	99
Accounts payable and other accrued expenses	1,605	1,663
	$ 2,217	$ 2,253

6. Short-Term Borrowings and Credit Arrangements

Loans and notes payable consist primarily of commercial paper issued in the United States. At December 31, 1993, the Company had $1.4 billion in lines of credit and other short-term credit facilities contractually available, under which $150 million was outstanding. Included were $1.0 billion in lines designated to support commercial paper and other borrowings, under which no amounts were outstanding at December 31, 1993. These facilities are subject to normal banking terms and conditions. Some of the financial arrangements require compensating balances, none of which are presently significant to the Company.

7. Accrued Taxes

Accrued taxes consist of the following (in millions):

December 31,	1993	1992
Income taxes	$ 1,106	$ 820
Sales, payroll and other taxes	176	143
	$ 1,282	$ 963

8. Long-Term Debt

Long-term debt consists of the following (in millions):

December 31,	1993	1992
7¾% U.S. dollar notes due 1996	$ 250	$ 250
5¾% Japanese yen notes due 1996	270	241
5¾% German mark notes due 1998[1]	147	156
7⅞% U.S. dollar notes due 1998	249	249
6⅝% U.S. dollar notes due 2002	149	149
6% U.S. dollar notes due 2003	150	—
7⅜% U.S. dollar notes due 2093	148	—
Other, due 1994 to 2013[2]	84	90
	1,447	1,135
Less current portion	19	15
	$ 1,428	$ 1,120

[1]Portions of these notes have been swapped for liabilities denominated in other currencies.
[2]The weighted average interest rate is approximately 7.8 percent.

Maturities of long-term debt for the five years succeeding December 31, 1993, are as follows (in millions):

1994	1995	1996	1997	1998
$19	$43	$527	$5	$400

The above notes include various restrictions, none of which are presently significant to the Company.

Interest paid was approximately $158 million, $174 million and $160 million in 1993, 1992 and 1991, respectively.

THE COCA-COLA COMPANY AND SUBSIDIARIES

NOTES TO CONSOLIDATED FINANCIAL STATEMENTS

9. Financial Instruments

The carrying amounts reflected in the consolidated balance sheets for cash, cash equivalents, loans and notes payable approximate the respective fair values due to the short maturities of these instruments. The fair values for marketable debt and equity securities, investments, receivables, long-term debt and hedging instruments are based primarily on quoted market prices for those or similar instruments. A comparison of the carrying value and fair value of these financial instruments is as follows (in millions):

December 31,	Carrying Value	Fair Value
1993		
Current marketable securities	$ 80	$ 102
Investments[1]	88	259
Finance subsidiary receivables	259	265
Marketable securities and other assets	868	865
Long-term debt	(1,447)	(1,531)
Hedging instruments	31	(142)
1992		
Current marketable securities	$ 107	$ 125
Investments[1]	258	300
Finance subsidiary receivables	126	135
Marketable securities and other assets	637	636
Long-term debt	(1,135)	(1,156)
Hedging instruments	102	99

[1]The consolidated balance sheet caption, Other, principally bottling companies, also includes equity investments of $1.0 billion and $839 million at December 31, 1993 and 1992, respectively.

Hedging transactions

The Company has entered into hedging transactions to reduce its exposure to adverse fluctuations in interest and foreign exchange rates. While the hedging instruments are subject to the risk of loss from changes in exchange rates, these losses would generally be offset by gains on the exposures being hedged. Realized and unrealized gains and losses on hedging instruments that are designated and effective as hedges of firmly committed foreign currency transactions are recognized in income in the same period as the hedged transaction. Approximately $9 million of losses realized on settled contracts entered into as hedges of firmly committed transactions in 1994, 1995 and 1996, were deferred at December 31, 1993.

From time to time, the Company purchases foreign currency option contracts to hedge anticipated transactions over the succeeding three years. Net unrealized gains/losses from hedging anticipated transactions were not material at December 31, 1993 or 1992.

At December 31, 1993 and 1992, the Company had forward exchange contracts, swaps, options and other financial market instruments, principally to exchange foreign currencies for U.S. dollars, of $4.6 billion and $4.9 billion, respectively. These amounts are representative of amounts maintained throughout 1993. Maturities of financial market instruments held at December 31, 1993, are as follows (in millions):

1994	1995	1996	1997 through 2003
$2,266	$753	$666	$961

Although pretax losses recognized on hedging transactions in 1993 amounted to $29 million, such losses were fully offset by income recognized on the exposures being hedged.

Guarantees

At December 31, 1993, the Company was contingently liable for guarantees of indebtedness owed by third parties of $140 million, of which $39 million is related to independent bottling licensees. In the opinion of management, it is not probable that the Company will be required to satisfy these guarantees. The fair value of these contingent liabilities is immaterial to the Company's consolidated financial statements.

10. Preferred Stock

The Company canceled the 3,000 issued shares of its $1 par value Cumulative Money Market Preferred Stock (MMP) in 1993 and returned the shares to the status of authorized but unissued shares. None of the MMP had been outstanding since 1991, when the final 750 shares of the 3,000 shares originally issued were redeemed.

11. Common Stock

Common shares outstanding and related changes for the three years ended December 31, 1993, are as follows (in millions):

	1993	1992	1991
Outstanding at January 1,	**1,307**	1,329	1,336
Issued to employees exercising stock options	**7**	9	4
Issued under restricted stock plans	**—**	—	3
Purchased for treasury			
Share repurchase programs	**(14)**	(30)	(14)
Stock option plan activity	**(3)**	(1)	—
Outstanding at December 31,	**1,297**	1,307	1,329

THE COCA-COLA COMPANY AND SUBSIDIARIES

NOTES TO CONSOLIDATED FINANCIAL STATEMENTS

12. Restricted Stock, Stock Options and Other Stock Plans

The Company sponsors restricted stock award plans, stock option plans, Incentive Unit Agreements and Performance Unit Agreements.

Under the amended 1989 Restricted Stock Award Plan and the amended 1983 Restricted Stock Award Plan (the Restricted Stock Plans), 20 million and 12 million shares of restricted common stock, respectively, may be granted to certain officers and key employees of the Company.

At December 31, 1993, 17 million shares were available for grant under the Restricted Stock Plans. The participant is entitled to vote and receive dividends on the shares, and, under the 1983 Restricted Stock Award Plan, the participant is reimbursed by the Company for income taxes imposed on the award, but not for taxes generated by the reimbursement payment. The shares are subject to certain transfer restrictions and may be forfeited if the participant leaves the Company for reasons other than retirement, disability or death, absent a change in control of the Company. On July 18, 1991, the Restricted Stock Plans were amended to specify age 62 as the minimum retirement age. The 1983 Restricted Stock Award Plan was further amended to conform to the terms of the 1989 Restricted Stock Award Plan by requiring a minimum of five years of service between the date of the award and retirement. The amendments affect shares granted after July 18, 1991.

Under the Company's 1991 Stock Option Plan (the Option Plan), a maximum of 60 million shares of the Company's common stock may be issued or transferred to certain officers and employees pursuant to stock options and stock appreciation rights granted under the Option Plan. The stock appreciation rights permit the holder, upon surrendering all or part of the related stock option, to receive cash, common stock or a combination thereof, in an amount up to 100 percent of the difference between the market price and the option price. No stock appreciation rights have been granted since 1990, and the Company presently does not intend to grant additional stock appreciation rights in the future. Options outstanding at December 31, 1993, also include various options granted under previous plans. Further information relating to options is as follows (in millions, except per share amounts):

	1993	1992	1991
Outstanding at January 1,	**31**	36	33
Granted	**6**	4	8
Exercised	**(7)**	(9)	(4)
Canceled	**—**	—	(1)
Outstanding at December 31,	**30**	31	36
Exercisable at December 31,	**22**	23	24
Shares available at December 31, for options that may be granted	**45**	51	55
Prices per share Exercised	**$4-$41**	$4-$28	$3-$28
Unexercised at December 31,	**$5-$44**	$4-$41	$4-$30

In 1988, the Company entered into Incentive Unit Agreements, whereby, subject to certain conditions, certain officers were given the right to receive cash awards based on the market value of 1.2 million shares of the Company's common stock at the measurement dates. Under the Incentive Unit Agreements, the employee is reimbursed by the Company for income taxes imposed when the value of the units is paid, but not for taxes generated by the reimbursement payment. As of December 31, 1993, 400,000 units have been paid and 800,000 units were outstanding.

In 1985, the Company entered into Performance Unit Agreements, whereby certain officers were given the right to receive cash awards based on the difference in the market value of approximately 2.2 million shares of the Company's common stock at the measurement dates and the base price of $5.16, the market value as of January 2, 1985. As of December 31, 1993, 780,000 units have been paid and approximately 1.4 million units were outstanding.

13. Pension Benefits

The Company sponsors and/or contributes to pension plans covering substantially all U.S. employees and certain employees in international locations. The benefits are primarily based on years of service and the employees' compensation for certain periods during the last years of employment. Pension costs are generally funded currently, subject to regulatory funding limitations. The Company also sponsors nonqualified, unfunded defined benefit plans for certain officers and other employees. In addition, the Company and its subsidiaries have various pension plans and other forms of postretirement arrangements outside the United States.

THE COCA-COLA COMPANY AND SUBSIDIARIES

NOTES TO CONSOLIDATED FINANCIAL STATEMENTS

Total pension expense for all benefit plans, including defined benefit plans, amounted to approximately $57 million in 1993, $49 million in 1992 and $42 million in 1991. Net periodic pension cost for the Company's defined benefit plans consists of the following (in millions):

	U.S. Plans			International Plans		
Year Ended December 31,	**1993**	1992	1991	**1993**	1992	1991
Service cost-benefits earned during the period	**$ 17**	$ 15	$ 13	**$ 17**	$ 18	$ 16
Interest cost on projected benefit obligation	**53**	50	46	**22**	20	18
Actual return on plan assets	**(77)**	(36)	(113)	**(27)**	(19)	(18)
Net amortization and deferral	**31**	(9)	71	**13**	3	1
Net periodic pension cost	**$ 24**	$ 20	$ 17	**$ 25**	$ 22	$ 17

The funded status for the Company's defined benefit plans is as follows (in millions):

	U.S. Plans				International Plans			
	Assets Exceed Accumulated Benefits		Accumulated Benefits Exceed Assets		Assets Exceed Accumulated Benefits		Accumulated Benefits Exceed Assets	
December 31,	**1993**	1992	**1993**	1992	**1993**	1992	**1993**	1992
Actuarial present value of benefit obligations								
Vested benefit obligation	**$ 481**	$ 401	**$ 109**	$ 82	**$ 139**	$ 119	**$ 110**	$ 90
Accumulated benefit obligation	**$ 523**	$ 431	**$ 111**	$ 89	**$ 151**	$ 127	**$ 126**	$ 100
Projected benefit obligation	**$ 598**	$ 520	**$ 133**	$ 101	**$ 196**	$ 167	**$ 177**	$ 148
Plan assets at fair value[1]	**631**	587	**2**	1	**200**	188	**94**	73
Plan assets in excess of (less than) projected benefit obligation	**33**	67	**(131)**[2]	(100)[2]	**4**	21	**(83)**	(75)
Unrecognized net (asset) liability at transition	**(34)**	(37)	**17**	19	**(16)**	(6)	**34**	33
Unrecognized prior service cost	**8**	23	**15**	3	**—**	—	**9**	8
Unrecognized net (gain) loss	**(24)**	(61)	**36**	24	**28**	2	**(3)**	(3)
Adjustment required to recognize minimum liability	**—**	—	**(46)**	(33)	**—**	—	**(7)**	(3)
Accrued pension asset (liability) included in the consolidated balance sheet	**$ (17)**	$ (8)	**$(109)**	$ (87)	**$ 16**	$ 17	**$ (50)**	$ (40)

[1]Primarily listed stocks, bonds and government securities.
[2]Substantially all of this amount relates to nonqualified, unfunded defined benefit plans.

The assumptions used in computing the preceding information are as follows:

	U.S. Plans			International Plans (weighted average rates)		
Year Ended December 31,	**1993**	1992	1991	**1993**	1992	1991
Discount rates	**7¼%**	8½%	9%	**6½%**	7%	7½%
Rates of increase in compensation levels	**4¾%**	6%	6%	**5%**	5½%	6%
Expected long-term rates of return on assets	**9½%**	9½%	9½%	**7%**	7%	7½%

NOTES TO CONSOLIDATED FINANCIAL STATEMENTS

14. Other Postretirement Benefits

The Company has plans providing postretirement health care and life insurance benefits to substantially all U.S. employees and certain employees in international locations who retire with a minimum of five years of service. The Company adopted SFAS 106 for all U.S. and international plans as of January 1, 1992. In 1992, the Company recorded an accumulated obligation for consolidated operations of $146 million, which is net of $92 million in deferred tax benefits. The Company also recorded an additional charge of $73 million, net of $13 million of deferred tax benefits, representing the Company's proportionate share of accumulated postretirement benefit obligations recognized by bottling investees accounted for by the equity method.

Net periodic cost for the Company's postretirement health care and life insurance benefits consists of the following (in millions):

Year Ended December 31,	1993	1992
Service cost	$10	$ 9
Interest cost	21	20
Other	(1)	—
	$30	$29

The Company contributes to a Voluntary Employees' Beneficiary Association trust that will be used to partially fund health care benefits for future retirees. The Company is funding benefits to the extent contributions are tax-deductible, which under current legislation is limited. In general, retiree health benefits are paid as covered expenses are incurred. The funded status for the Company's postretirement health care and life insurance plans is as follows (in millions):

December 31,	1993	1992
Accumulated postretirement benefit obligations:		
Retirees	$ 132	$ 111
Fully eligible active plan participants	35	34
Other active plan participants	131	113
Total benefit obligation	298	258
Plan assets at fair value[1]	42	24
Plan assets less than benefit obligation	(256)	(234)
Unrecognized net loss	23	—
Accrued postretirement benefit liability included in the consolidated balance sheet	$(233)	$(234)

[1] Consists of corporate bonds, government securities and short-term investments.

The assumptions used in computing the preceding information are as follows:

Year Ended December 31,	1993	1992
Discount Rate	7¼%	8½%
Rate of increase in compensation levels	4¾%	6%

The rate of increase in the per capita costs of covered health care benefits is assumed to be 11 percent in 1994, decreasing gradually to 5½ percent by the year 2005. Increasing the assumed health care cost trend rate by 1 percentage point would increase the accumulated postretirement benefit obligation as of December 31, 1993, by approximately $35 million and increase net periodic postretirement benefit cost by approximately $4 million in 1993.

15. Income Taxes

Income before income taxes and changes in accounting principles consists of the following (in millions):

Year Ended December 31,	1993	1992	1991
United States	$ 1,035	$ 762	$ 648
International	2,150	1,984	1,735
	$ 3,185	$2,746	$2,383

Income tax expense (benefit) consists of the following (in millions):

Year Ended December 31,	United States	State & Local	International	Total
1993				
Current	$356	$ 34	$669	$1,059
Deferred[1]	(64)	5	(3)	(62)
1992				
Current	$ 278	$ 36	$ 576	$ 890
Deferred[1]	(60)	(1)	34	(27)
1991				
Current	$ 233	$ 31	$ 595	$ 859
Deferred	(89)	(5)	—	(94)

[1] Additional deferred tax benefits of $8 million in 1993 and $105 million in 1992 have been included in the SFAS 112 and SFAS 106 transition effect charges, respectively.

The Company made income tax payments of approximately $650 million, $856 million and $672 million in 1993, 1992 and 1991, respectively.

THE COCA-COLA COMPANY AND SUBSIDIARIES

NOTES TO CONSOLIDATED FINANCIAL STATEMENTS

A reconciliation of the statutory U.S. federal rate and effective rates is as follows:

Year Ended December 31,	1993	1992	1991
Statutory U.S. federal rate	35.0%	34.0%	34.0%
State income taxes-net of federal benefit	1.0	1.0	1.0
Earnings in jurisdictions taxed at rates different from the statutory U.S. federal rate	(5.1)	(3.8)	(3.1)
Equity income	(1.7)	(1.0)	(.6)
Other–net	2.1	1.2	.8
	31.3%	31.4%	32.1%

The tax effects of temporary differences and carryforwards that give rise to significant portions of deferred tax assets and liabilities consist of the following (in millions):

December 31,	1993	1992
Deferred tax assets:		
Benefit plans	$298	$297
Liabilities and reserves	177	119
Net operating loss carryforwards	141	101
Other	120	84
Gross deferred tax assets	736	601
Valuation allowance	(75)	(63)
Total	$661	$538
Deferred tax liabilities:		
Property, plant and equipment	$342	$312
Equity investments	180	197
Intangible assets	52	68
Other	61	43
Total	$635	$620
Net deferred tax asset (liability)[1]	$ 26	$ (82)

[1]Deferred tax assets of $139 million have been included in the consolidated balance sheet caption marketable securities and other assets at December 31, 1993.

At December 31, 1993, the Company had $403 million of operating loss carryforwards available to reduce future taxable income of certain international subsidiaries. Loss carryforwards of $293 million must be utilized within the next five years, and $110 million can be utilized over an indefinite period. A valuation allowance has been provided for a portion of the deferred tax assets related to these loss carryforwards.

As the result of changes in U.S. tax law, the Company was required to record charges for additional taxes and tax-related expenses that reduced net income by approximately $51 million in 1993. The Company's effective tax rate reflects the favorable U.S. tax treatment from manufacturing facilities in Puerto Rico that operate under a negotiated exemption grant that expires December 31, 2009, as well as the tax benefit derived from significant operations outside the United States, which are taxed at rates lower than the U.S. statutory rate of 35 percent. Changes to U.S. tax law enacted in 1993 will limit the utilization of the favorable tax treatment from operations in Puerto Rico beginning in 1994, and will exert upward pressure on the Company's effective tax rate.

Appropriate U.S. and international taxes have been provided for earnings of subsidiary companies that are expected to be remitted to the parent company. The cumulative amount of unremitted earnings of international subsidiaries that are expected to be indefinitely reinvested, exclusive of amounts that, if remitted, would result in little or no tax, is approximately $426 million at December 31, 1993. The taxes that would be paid upon remittance of these earnings are approximately $149 million.

16. Net Change in Operating Assets and Liabilities

The changes in operating assets and liabilities, net of effects of acquisitions and divestitures of businesses and unrealized exchange gains/losses, are as follows (in millions):

Year Ended December 31,	1993	1992	1991
Increase in trade accounts receivable	$(151)	$(147)	$ (32)
Increase in inventories	(41)	(138)	(3)
Increase in prepaid expenses and other assets	(76)	(112)	(326)
Increase (decrease) in accounts payable and accrued expenses	(44)	405	267
Increase in accrued taxes	355	57	244
Increase (decrease) in other liabilities	11	(108)	101
	$ 54	$ (43)	$ 251

THE COCA-COLA COMPANY AND SUBSIDIARIES

NOTES TO CONSOLIDATED FINANCIAL STATEMENTS

17. Acquisitions and Investments

During 1993, the Company's acquisition and investment activity, which includes investments in bottling operations in Mexico, Belgium and the United States, totaled $816 million. During 1992 and 1991, the Company's acquisition and investment activity totaled $717 million and $399 million, respectively. None of the acquisitions in 1992 or 1991 were individually significant.

As discussed in Note 3, the Company purchased bottling operations in Tennessee that were subsequently sold to Coca-Cola Enterprises along with a bottling operation in the Netherlands. Note 3 also includes a discussion of the Company's 1993 investments in bottling operations in Mexico and in the United States.

The acquisitions have been accounted for by the purchase method of accounting, and, accordingly, their results have been included in the consolidated financial statements from their respective dates of acquisition. Had the results of these businesses been included in operations commencing with 1991, the reported results would not have been materially affected.

18. Nonrecurring Items

Upon a favorable court decision in 1993, the Company reversed the previously recorded reserves for bottler litigation, resulting in a $13 million reduction to selling, administrative and general expenses and a $10 million reduction to interest expense. Selling, administrative and general expenses for 1993 also include provisions of $63 million to increase efficiencies in European, domestic and corporate operations. Also in 1993, equity income has been reduced by $42 million related to restructuring charges recorded by Coca-Cola Beverages Ltd. Other income (deductions)-net includes a $50 million pretax gain recorded by the foods business sector upon the sale of citrus groves in the United States, and a $34 million pretax gain recognized on the sale of property no longer required as a result of a consolidation of manufacturing operations in Japan.

Other income (deductions)-net in 1991 includes a $69 million pretax gain on the sale of property no longer required as a result of consolidating manufacturing operations in Japan and a $27 million pretax gain on the sale of the Company's 22 percent ownership interest in Johnston to Coca-Cola Enterprises. Selling, administrative and

general expenses and interest expense in 1991 include the original charges of $13 million and $8 million, respectively, for bottler litigation reversed in 1993. In addition, 1991 equity income has been reduced by $44 million related to restructuring charges recorded by Coca-Cola Enterprises.

Net Operating Revenues by Line of Business

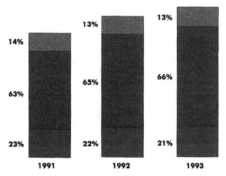

Operating Income by Line of Business

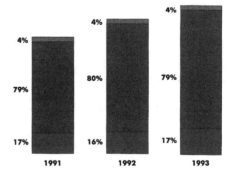

THE COCA-COLA COMPANY AND SUBSIDIARIES

NOTES TO CONSOLIDATED FINANCIAL STATEMENTS

19. Lines of Business

The Company operates in two major lines of business: soft drinks and foods (principally juice and juice-drink products).
Information concerning operations in these businesses is as follows (in millions):

| | Soft Drinks | | | | |
	United States	International	Foods	Corporate	Consolidated
1993					
Net operating revenues	$2,966	$9,205	$1,766	$ 20	$13,957
Operating income	618[1]	2,753[1]	127	(396)[1]	3,102
Identifiable operating assets	1,956	5,809	761	1,280[3]	9,806
Equity income				91[1]	91
Investments (principally bottling companies)				2,215	2,215
Capital expenditures	136	557	30	77	800
Depreciation and amortization	91	172	38	59	360
1992					
Net operating revenues	$2,813	$8,551	$1,675	$ 35	$13,074
Operating income	510	2,521	112	(373)	2,770
Identifiable operating assets	1,812	5,251	791	1,035[3]	8,889
Equity income				65	65
Investments (principally bottling companies)				2,163	2,163
Capital expenditures	169	736	38	140	1,083
Depreciation and amortization	87	157	35	43	322
1991					
Net operating revenues	$2,645	$7,245	$1,636	$ 46	$11,572
Operating income	469	2,141	104	(395)	2,319
Identifiable operating assets	1,447	4,742	755	1,124[3]	8,068
Equity income				40[2]	40
Investments (principally bottling companies)				2,121	2,121
Capital expenditures	131	547	57	57	792
Depreciation and amortization	82	112	30	37	261

Intercompany transfers between sectors are not material.

[1] Operating income for soft drink operations in the United States, International operations and Corporate were reduced by $13 million, $33 million and $17 million, respectively, for provisions to increase efficiencies. Equity income was reduced by $42 million related to restructuring charges recorded by Coca-Cola Beverages Ltd.
[2] Reduced by $44 million related to restructuring charges recorded by Coca-Cola Enterprises.
[3] Corporate identifiable operating assets are composed principally of marketable securities and fixed assets.

| Compound Growth Rates Ending 1993 | Soft Drinks | | | |
	United States	International	Foods	Consolidated
Net operating revenues				
5 years	8%	15%	3%	12%
10 years	7%	14%	5%	11%
Operating income				
5 years	12%	16%	7%	14%
10 years	10%	17%	1%	14%

THE COCA-COLA COMPANY AND SUBSIDIARIES

NOTES TO CONSOLIDATED FINANCIAL STATEMENTS

20. Operations in Geographic Areas

Information about the Company's operations in different geographic areas is as follows (in millions):

	United States	Africa	European Community	Latin America	Northeast Europe/ Middle East	Pacific & Canada	Corporate	Consolidated
1993								
Net operating revenues	$ 4,586	$ 255	$ 3,834	$ 1,683	$ 677	$ 2,902	$ 20	$ 13,957
Operating income	730[1]	152	872[1]	582	152	1,010	(396)[1]	3,102
Identifiable operating assets	2,682	153	2,777	1,220	604	1,090	1,280[3]	9,806
Equity income							91[1]	91
Investments (principally bottling companies)							2,215	2,215
Capital expenditures	165	6	239	141	129	43	77	800
Depreciation and amortization	127	3	99	33	22	17	59	360
1992[4]								
Net operating revenues	$ 4,339	$ 242	$ 3,984	$ 1,383	$ 546	$ 2,545	$ 35	$ 13,074
Operating income	608	129	889	502	108	907	(373)	2,770
Identifiable operating assets	2,563	139	2,587	1,185	435	945	1,035[3]	8,889
Equity income							65	65
Investments (principally bottling companies)							2,163	2,163
Capital expenditures	204	12	386	188	120	33	140	1,083
Depreciation and amortization	121	3	99	27	14	15	43	322
1991[4]								
Net operating revenues	$ 4,125	$ 206	$ 3,338	$ 1,103	$ 408	$ 2,346	$ 46	$ 11,572
Operating income	560	105	768	405	99	777	(395)	2,319
Identifiable operating assets	2,161	126	2,558	815	297	987	1,124[3]	8,068
Equity income							40[2]	40
Investments (principally bottling companies)							2,121	2,121
Capital expenditures	185	6	331	106	55	52	57	792
Depreciation and amortization	111	2	66	23	7	15	37	261

Intercompany transfers between geographic areas are not material.
Identifiable liabilities of operations outside the United States amounted to approximately $1.9 billion at December 31, 1993 and 1992, and $1.8 billion at December 31, 1991.

[1]Operating income for the United States, European Community and Corporate were reduced by $13 million, $33 million and $17 million, respectively, for provisions to increase efficiencies. Equity income was reduced by $42 million related to restructuring charges recorded by Coca-Cola Beverages Ltd.
[2]Reduced by $44 million related to restructuring charges recorded by Coca-Cola Enterprises.
[3]Corporate identifiable operating assets are composed principally of marketable securities and fixed assets.
[4]In 1993, the Company divided its Northeast Europe/Africa group into the Northeast Europe/Middle East and Africa groups. Accordingly, previous years' results have been reclassified to reflect this change.

Compound Growth Rates Ending 1993	United States	Africa	European Community	Latin America	Northeast Europe/ Middle East	Pacific & Canada	Consolidated
Net operating revenues							
5 years	6%	11%	19%	24%	24%	7%	12%
10 years	6%	(4)%	18%	15%	21%	13%	11%
Operating income							
5 years	11%	20%	13%	27%	17%	12%	14%
10 years	8%	2%	19%	24%	22%	18%	14%

THE COCA-COLA COMPANY AND SUBSIDIARIES

REPORT OF INDEPENDENT AUDITORS

Net Operating Revenues by Geographic Area

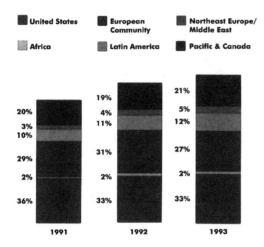

Operating Income by Geographic Area

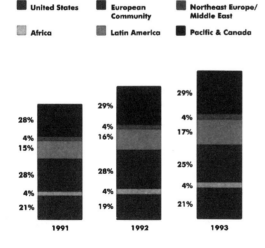

**Board of Directors and Share Owners
The Coca-Cola Company**

We have audited the accompanying consolidated balance sheets of The Coca-Cola Company and subsidiaries as of December 31, 1993 and 1992, and the related consolidated statements of income, share-owners' equity and cash flows for each of the three years in the period ended December 31, 1993. These financial statements are the responsibility of the Company's management. Our responsibility is to express an opinion on these financial statements based on our audits.

We conducted our audits in accordance with generally accepted auditing standards. Those standards require that we plan and perform the audit to obtain reasonable assurance about whether the financial statements are free of material misstatement. An audit includes examining, on a test basis, evidence supporting the amounts and disclosures in the financial statements. An audit also includes assessing the accounting principles used and significant estimates made by management, as well as evaluating the overall financial statement presentation. We believe that our audits provide a reasonable basis for our opinion.

In our opinion, the financial statements referred to above present fairly, in all material respects, the consolidated financial position of The Coca-Cola Company and subsidiaries at December 31, 1993 and 1992, and the consolidated results of their operations and their cash flows for each of the three years in the period ended December 31, 1993, in conformity with generally accepted accounting principles.

As discussed in Note 1 to the consolidated financial statements, in 1993 the Company changed its method of accounting for postemployment benefits. As discussed in Note 14 to the consolidated financial statements, in 1992 the Company changed its method of accounting for postretirement benefits other than pensions.

Ernst & Young

Atlanta, Georgia
January 25, 1994

THE COCA-COLA COMPANY AND SUBSIDIARIES

REPORT OF MANAGEMENT

Management is responsible for the preparation and integrity of the consolidated financial statements appearing in this Annual Report. The financial statements were prepared in conformity with generally accepted accounting principles appropriate in the circumstances and, accordingly, include some amounts based on management's best judgments and estimates. Financial information in this Annual Report is consistent with that in the financial statements.

Management is responsible for maintaining a system of internal accounting controls and procedures to provide reasonable assurance, at an appropriate cost/benefit relationship, that assets are safeguarded and that transactions are authorized, recorded and reported properly. The internal accounting control system is augmented by a program of internal audits and appropriate reviews by management, written policies and guidelines, careful selection and training of qualified personnel and a written Code of Business Conduct adopted by the Board of Directors, applicable to all employees of the Company and its subsidiaries. Management believes that the Company's internal accounting controls provide reasonable assurance that assets are safeguarded against material loss from unauthorized use or disposition and that the financial records are reliable for preparing financial statements and other data and for maintaining accountability of assets.

The Audit Committee of the Board of Directors, composed solely of Directors who are not officers of the Company, meets with the independent auditors, management and internal auditors periodically to discuss internal accounting controls and auditing and financial reporting matters. The Committee reviews with the independent auditors the scope and results of the audit effort. The Committee also meets with the independent auditors and the chief internal auditor without management present to ensure that the independent auditors and the chief internal auditor have free access to the Committee.

The independent auditors, Ernst & Young, are recommended by the Audit Committee of the Board of Directors, selected by the Board of Directors and ratified by the share owners. Ernst & Young is engaged to audit the consolidated financial statements of The Coca-Cola Company and subsidiaries and conduct such tests and related procedures as it deems necessary in conformity with generally accepted auditing standards. The opinion of the independent auditors, based upon their audits of the consolidated financial statements, is contained in this Annual Report.

Roberto C. Goizueta
Chairman, Board of Directors,
and Chief Executive Officer

Jack L. Stahl
Senior Vice President
and Chief Financial Officer

James E. Chestnut
Vice President
and Controller

January 25, 1994

THE COCA-COLA COMPANY AND SUBSIDIARIES

QUARTERLY DATA (UNAUDITED)

For the years ended December 31, 1993 and 1992
(In millions except per share data)

1993	First Quarter	Second Quarter	Third Quarter	Fourth Quarter	Full Year
Net operating revenues	$ 3,056	$ 3,899	$ 3,629	$ 3,373	$13,957
Gross profit	1,963	2,435	2,286	2,113	8,797
Income before change in accounting principle	454	678	590	466	2,188
Net income	442	678	590	466	2,176
Income per share before change in accounting principle	.35	.52	.45	.36	1.68
Net income per share	.34	.52	.45	.36	1.67

1992	First Quarter	Second Quarter	Third Quarter	Fourth Quarter	Full Year
Net operating revenues	$ 2,772	$ 3,550	$ 3,508	$ 3,244	$13,074
Gross profit	1,740	2,177	2,122	1,980	8,019
Income before change in accounting principle	386	565	540	392	1,883
Net income	167	565	540	392	1,664
Income per share before change in accounting principle	.29	.43	.41	.30	1.43
Net income per share	.13	.43	.41	.30	1.26

The Company filed a Form 8-K with the Securities and Exchange Commission in January 1994 restating the 1993 quarterly reports for the adoption of a change in accounting for postemployment benefits. The after-tax transition charge related to the restatement reduced first quarter net income by $12 million ($.01 per share).

The third quarter of 1993 includes an after-tax impact of $47 million due to changes in U.S. tax law which reduced full year after-tax income by $51 million ($.04 per share) and the reversal of previously recorded reserves for bottler litigation of $23 million ($.01 per share after income taxes).

The fourth quarter of 1993 includes provisions to increase efficiencies of $63 million ($.03 per share after income taxes), a reduction of $42 million ($.02 per share after income taxes) related to restructuring charges by an equity investee, a gain from the sale of real estate in Japan ($34 million, or $.02 per share after income taxes), a gain from the sale of citrus groves in the United States ($50 million, or $.02 per share after income taxes) and a gain recognized on the issuance of stock by an equity investee of $12 million ($.01 per share after income taxes).

The first quarter of 1992 includes the after-tax transition charge of $219 million related to the change in accounting for postretirement benefits other than pensions. This charge decreased net income per share by $.16 for the quarter and $.17 for the year. The sum of net income per share for the four quarters was $.01 higher than the reported full year amount due to rounding.

Stock Prices

Below are the New York Stock Exchange high, low and closing prices of The Coca-Cola Company stock for each quarter of 1993 and 1992.

1993	First Quarter	Second Quarter	Third Quarter	Fourth Quarter
High	$ 44.13	$ 43.63	$ 44.75	$ 45.13
Low	40.00	37.50	41.75	40.00
Close	42.63	43.00	42.25	44.63

1992	First Quarter	Second Quarter	Third Quarter	Fourth Quarter
High	$ 41.69	$ 45.13	$ 45.38	$ 44.50
Low	35.56	38.88	39.75	36.50
Close	40.88	40.00	40.50	41.88

John H. Harland Company and Subsidiaries

JOHN H. HARLAND COMPANY AND SUBSIDIARIES

Consolidated **Statements Of Income**	YEAR ENDED DECEMBER 31		
	1993	**1992**	**1991**
(IN THOUSANDS EXCEPT PER SHARE AMOUNTS)			
NET SALES	$ 519,486	$ 444,980	$ 378,659
COST AND EXPENSES:			
Cost of sales	288,786	236,559	189,835
Selling, general and administrative expenses	125,077	111,100	94,060
Employees' profit sharing	9,614	9,118	8,105
Amortization of intangibles	8,702	4,673	
Restructuring charge			12,191
Total	432,179	361,450	304,191
INCOME FROM OPERATIONS	87,307	83,530	74,468
INTEREST AND OTHER INCOME (EXPENSE)-NET	(1,633)	4,737	5,234
INCOME BEFORE INCOME TAXES AND CUMULATIVE EFFECT OF CHANGE IN ACCOUNTING PRINCIPLE	85,674	88,267	79,702
INCOME TAXES	33,152	31,629	29,882
INCOME BEFORE CUMULATIVE EFFECT OF CHANGE IN ACCOUNTING PRINCIPLE	52,522	56,638	49,820
CUMULATIVE EFFECT OF CHANGE IN ACCOUNTING PRINCIPLE			2,385
NET INCOME	$ 52,522	$ 56,638	$ 47,435
PER COMMON SHARE:			
Income before cumulative effect of change in accounting principle	$ 1.62	$ 1.59	$ 1.33
Net Income	$ 1.62	$ 1.59	$ 1.27

See Notes to Consolidated Financial Statements.

 HARLAND'S 1993 FINANCIAL STATEMENTS ARE PRINTED ON RECYCLED PAPER.

	DECEMBER 31	
Consolidated Balance Sheets	**1993**	**1992**

(IN THOUSANDS EXCEPT SHARE AND PER SHARE AMOUNTS)

ASSETS

CURRENT ASSETS:

	1993	1992
Cash and cash equivalents	$ 26,224	$ 19,133
Short-term investments	1,900	150
Accounts receivable from customers, less allowance for doubtful accounts of $1,753 and $1,343	63,660	56,700
Inventories:		
Raw materials and semi-finished goods	22,389	20,692
Hardware component parts	1,478	2,547
Finished goods	2,133	3,882
Deferred income taxes	6,694	
Other	10,417	7,555
Total current assets	134,895	110,659
INVESTMENTS AND OTHER ASSETS:		
Investments	8,103	7,705
Goodwill and other intangibles - net	54,053	37,528
Acquisition deposit and other	7,014	36,259
Total investments and other assets	69,170	81,492
PROPERTY, PLANT AND EQUIPMENT:		
Land	9,201	8,746
Buildings and improvements	72,212	66,394
Machinery and equipment	204,405	186,400
Furniture and fixtures	15,082	13,259
Leasehold improvements	2,134	2,050
Additions in progress	2,008	1,434
Total	305,042	278,283
Less accumulated depreciation and amortization	152,656	130,554
Property, plant and equipment - net	152,386	147,729
TOTAL	$356,451	$ 339,880

See Notes to Consolidated Financial Statements.

JOHN H. HARLAND COMPANY AND SUBSIDIARIES

DECEMBER 31

	1993	1992
LIABILITIES AND SHAREHOLDERS' EQUITY		
CURRENT LIABILITIES:		
Short-term debt	$ 4,000	$ 22,000
Accounts payable - trade	8,690	9,639
Accrued liabilities:		
Salaries, wages and employee benefits	15,458	11,966
Taxes	649	4,090
Other	15,182	11,771
Total current liabilities	43,979	59,466
LONG-TERM LIABILITIES:		
Long-term debt	111,542	12,622
Deferred income taxes	6,393	1,987
Other	10,863	9,583
Total long-term liabilities	128,798	24,192
Total liabilities	172,777	83,658
SHAREHOLDERS' EQUITY:		
Series preferred stock, authorized 500,000 shares of $1.00 par value, none issued		
Common stock, authorized 144,000,000 shares of $1.00 par value, 37,907,497 shares issued	37,907	37,907
Additional paid-in capital	4,225	4,326
Foreign currency translation adjustment	72	187
Retained earnings	325,323	303,249
Total shareholders' equity	367,527	345,669
Less 7,421,903 and 3,858,049 shares in treasury, at cost	183,853	89,447
Shareholders' equity - net	183,674	256,222
TOTAL	$ 356,451	$ 339,880

	YEAR ENDED DECEMBER 31		
Consolidated Statements of Cash Flows (IN THOUSANDS)	**1993**	**1992**	**1991**
OPERATING ACTIVITIES:			
Net Income	$ 52,522	$ 56,638	$ 47,435
Adjustments to reconcile net income to net cash provided by operating activities:			
Depreciation and amortization	35,102	29,662	22,684
Deferred income taxes	(2,288)	(2,135)	(5,767)
Loss (gain) on sale of assets	599	(3,410)	
Provision for restructuring charge			12,191
Provision for postretirement benefits	768	640	4,156
Other	965	1,070	1,915
Change in assets and liabilities net of effects of businesses acquired:			
Accounts receivable	3,059	(3,706)	6,740
Inventories and other current assets	3,347	1,540	(1,398)
Accounts payable and accrued expenses	(2,969)	(2,142)	5,502
Other - net	(434)	229	(238)
Net cash provided by operating activities	90,671	78,386	93,220
INVESTING ACTIVITIES:			
Purchases of property, plant and equipment	(27,121)	(18,721)	(16,899)
Proceeds from sale of property, plant and equipment	1,474	1,979	1,059
Change in short-term investments - net	(1,750)	52,350	(32,465)
Payment for acquisition of businesses - net of cash acquired	(9,564)	(54,826)	
Acquisition deposit		(31,900)	
Proceeds from sale of Puerto Rico bonds		49,982	
Other - net	(2,469)	(2,169)	1,989
Net cash used in investing activities	(39,430)	(3,305)	(46,316)
FINANCING ACTIVITIES:			
Proceeds from issuance of long-term debt	100,000		
Short-term borrowings	(18,000)	18,000	
Purchases of treasury stock	(99,435)	(65,565)	(22,806)
Issuance of treasury stock	4,779	4,818	4,061
Dividends paid	(30,448)	(32,088)	(32,196)
Other - net	(1,046)	(36)	806
Net cash used in financing activities	(44,150)	(74,871)	(50,135)
Increase (decrease) in cash and cash equivalents	7,091	210	(3,231)
Cash and cash equivalents at beginning of year	19,133	18,923	22,154
Cash and cash equivalents at end of year	$ 26,224	$ 19,133	$ 18,923
Cash paid during the year for:			
Interest	$ 2,144	$ 998	$ 1,115
Income taxes	$ 38,785	$ 36,613	$ 31,972

See Notes to Consolidated Financial Statements.

JOHN H. HARLAND COMPANY AND SUBSIDIARIES

Consolidated Statements of Shareholders' Equity

YEARS ENDED DECEMBER 31, 1993, 1992 AND 1991

(IN THOUSANDS EXCEPT SHARE AND PER SHARE AMOUNTS)

	Common Stock	Additional Paid-In Capital	Retained Earnings	Treasury Stock	Foreign Currency Translation Adjustments
BALANCE, DECEMBER 31, 1990	$ 37,907	$ 5,661	$ 263,460	$ (11,845)	$ 503
Net Income			47,435		
Cash dividends, $.86 per share			(32,196)		
Purchase of 1,024,213 shares of treasury stock				(22,806)	
Issuance of 238,235 shares of treasury stock under employee stock plans		(1,253)		5,272	
Foreign currency translation adjustment					(197)
Other		285		37	
BALANCE, DECEMBER 31, 1991	37,907	4,693	278,699	(29,342)	306
Net Income			56,638		
Cash dividends, $.90 per share			(32,088)		
Purchase of 2,781,813 shares of treasury stock				(65,565)	
Issuance of 261,308 shares of treasury stock under employee stock plans		(642)		5,460	
Foreign currency translation adjustment					(119)
Other		275			
BALANCE, DECEMBER 31, 1992	37,907	4,326	303,249	(89,447)	187
Net Income			52,522		
Cash dividends, $.94 per share			(30,448)		
Purchase of 3,792,377 shares of treasury stock				(99,435)	
Issuance of 228,523 shares of treasury stock under employee stock plans		(250)		5,029	
Foreign currency translation adjustment					(115)
Other		149			
BALANCE, DECEMBER 31, 1993	$ 37,907	$ 4,225	$ 325,323	$ (183,853)	$ 72

See Notes to Consolidated Financial Statements.

To Consolidated Financial Statements

1. SIGNIFICANT ACCOUNTING POLICIES:

Consolidation - The consolidated financial statements include the financial statements of John H. Harland Company and its wholly owned subsidiaries (the "Company"). Intercompany balances and transactions have been eliminated.

Cash Equivalents - The Company considers all highly liquid debt instruments purchased with a maturity of three months or less to be cash equivalents.

Inventories - Inventories are stated at the lower of cost or market. Cost of inventory for checks and related forms is determined by average costing. Cost of scannable forms and hardware component parts inventories is determined by the first-in, first-out method. Cost of data entry terminals is determined by the specific identification method.

Investments - Short-term investments are carried at cost plus accrued interest, which approximates market, and consist primarily of certificates of deposit and demand notes with original maturities in excess of three months. Marketable equity securities included in long-term investments are carried at the lower of cost or market. Other long-term investments are carried principally at cost.

Property, Plant and Equipment - Property, plant and equipment are carried at cost. Depreciation of buildings is computed primarily by the declining balance method. Depreciation of equipment, furniture and fixtures is calculated by the straight-line or sum-of-the-years digits methods. Leasehold improvements are amortized by the straight-line method over the life of the lease or the life of the property, whichever is shorter. Accelerated methods are used for income tax purposes for all property where it is allowed.

Goodwill and Other Intangibles - Amortization of goodwill is calculated by the straight-line method over a 40-year period. The Company periodically assesses the recoverability of goodwill based on its judgment as to the future profitability of its operations. Other intangible assets consist primarily of purchased customer lists and non-compete covenants. Amortization of other intangible assets is calculated by the straight-line method over the estimated useful life which is primarily a 5-year period.

Net Income Per Share - Net income per common share is based on the weighted average number of shares of common stock and common share equivalents outstanding during each year which was 32,460,128 for 1993, 35,688,645 for 1992 and 37,468,637 for 1991. Common share equivalents include the number of shares issuable upon the exercise of the Company's stock options and the conversion of convertible securities. The difference between primary and fully diluted common share equivalents is not significant.

Income Taxes - Effective Jan. 1, 1993, the Company adopted Statement of Financial Accounting Standards No. 109, "Accounting for Income Taxes" ("SFAS 109") in which deferred tax liabilities and assets are determined based on the difference between financial statements and tax bases of assets and liabilities using enacted tax rates in effect for the year in which the differences are expected to reverse.

2. BUSINESS SEGMENTS: The Company operates principally within the printing industry.

3. ACQUISITIONS: On January 1, 1993, the Company completed the acquisition of substantially all the net assets of the Denver-based Rocky Mountain Bank Note Company ("RMBN") for cash of $37.9 million and acquisition related costs of approximately $8.9 million. The purchase was funded through short-term borrowings of $18.0 million and by internally generated funds. The acquisition has been accounted for as a purchase and, accordingly, the acquired net assets and operations have been included in the consolidated financial statements from the date of acquisition. Assets acquired totaled $46.8 million, net of liabilities assumed of $2.0 million. Of the total acquisition cost, $25.7 million was allocated to intangible assets, of which $10.7 million represented goodwill.

On February 19, 1992, the Company completed the acquisition of substantially all the net assets of

Interchecks Inc. ("Interchecks"), a Seattle, Washington-based check printer for a cash purchase price of $50 million and acquisition related costs of $9.4 million. The acquisition has been accounted for as a purchase and, accordingly, the acquired net assets and operations have been included in the consolidated financial statements from the date of acquisition. Assets acquired totaled $59.4 million, net of liabilities assumed of $4.7 million. Of the total acquisition cost, $38.4 million was allocated to intangible assets, of which $13.4 million represented goodwill.

The following represents the unaudited pro forma results of operations which assumes the acquisitions occurred at the beginning of the respective year in which the assets were acquired as well as the beginning of the immediately preceding year. These results include certain adjustments, primarily increased amortization of intangible assets, reduced interest income and reduced depreciation expense (in thousands of dollars, except per share amounts):

	1992	1991
Net sales	$ 539,889	$ 453,541
Income before cumulative effect of change in accounting principle	55,968	45,938
Net income	55,968	43,553
Per common share:		
Income before cumulative effect of change in accounting principle	1.57	1.21
Net income	1.57	1.15

The pro forma financial information presented above does not purport to be indicative of either the results of operations that would have occurred had the acquisitions taken place at the beginning of the periods presented or of future results of operations of the combined businesses.

4. RESTRUCTURING CHARGE: During the fourth quarter of 1991, the Company recorded a provision of $12,191,000 for the restructuring and revaluation of certain subsidiaries and investments of $9,191,000 and for taxes of $3,000,000 for the repatriation of earnings from Puerto Rico. The Company's policy had been to invest such earnings

long term to avoid the payment of taxes upon repatriation.

5. INVESTMENTS AND OTHER ASSETS: Long-term investments at December 31, 1993 primarily consisted of investments in limited partnerships.

Other assets at December 31, 1992 included a $31,900,000 deposit related to the acquisition of RMBN.

6. SHORT-TERM DEBT: At December 31, 1993, the Company had available unsecured lines of credit under which it could borrow up to $111,000,000 in the form of short-term notes for which no compensating balances or commitment fees are required. At December 31, 1992, the Company had borrowed $18,000,000 under the lines of credit at an interest rate of 3.8%. No amounts were outstanding under the lines of credit at December 31, 1993.

In addition, the Company had outstanding at December 31, 1993 and 1992 an Industrial Revenue Bond, due on demand, in the amount of $4,000,000 which bears interest at an average rate of 5.26%.

7. LONG-TERM DEBT: The Company's long-term debt consists of (in thousands):

	1993	1992
Series A Senior Notes	$ 85,000	
Term Loan	15,000	
Convertible Subordinated Debentures	10,600	$ 10,579
Other	1,477	2,573
	112,077	13,152
Less current portion	535	530
Long-term debt	$111,542	$ 12,622

In December 1993, the Company issued $85,000,000 of Series A Senior Notes ("Senior Notes") and arranged a $15,000,000 Term Loan ("Term Loan"). The Senior Notes and the Term Loan are at fixed interest rates of 6.60% and 6.63%, respectively. The Senior Notes mature from 2004 to 2008 and the Term Loan is due 2003. Both the Term Loan and the Senior Notes contain certain covenants, the most restrictive of

Notes (continued)

which limit the amount of funded indebtedness of the Company and require the Company to maintain a minimum fixed charge coverage ratio. At December 31, 1993, the Company was in compliance with the covenants associated with these agreements.

The Company's 6.75% convertible subordinated debentures are convertible into common stock of the Company at any time prior to maturity, at a conversion price of $25.17 per share, subject to adjustment in certain events. At December 31, 1993, there were 328,249 shares of common stock reserved for conversion of the debentures. The debentures are entitled to an annual mandatory sinking fund, commencing June 1, 1996, calculated to retire 75% of the debentures prior to maturity in 2011. The debentures are redeemable, in whole or in part, at any time at the option of the Company at specific redemption prices plus accrued interest. The debentures are subordinated to all senior debt.

Other long-term debt relates principally to capitalized lease obligations.

Annual maturities of long-term debt including sinking fund requirements during the next five years are: 1994-$535,000; 1995-$519,000; 1996-$813,000; 1997-$559,000; and 1998-$550,000.

8. INCOME TAXES: Effective January 1, 1993, the Company adopted SFAS 109. Previously, the Company had computed its income tax expense in accordance with the provisions of the Accounting Principles Board Opinion No. 11. The cumulative effect of adopting SFAS 109 was not significant to the Company's consolidated financial statements. The provision for income taxes for the years ended December 31, 1993, 1992 and 1991 (including the impact of the accounting change in 1991) includes the following (in thousands):

	1993	1992	1991
Current:			
Federal	$ 28,350	$ 29,709	$ 29,259
State	7,090	4,055	4,959
Total	35,440	33,764	34,218
Deferred:			
Federal	(1,999)	(1,879)	(5,254)
State	(289)	(256)	(513)
Total	(2,288)	(2,135)	(5,767)
Total	$ 33,152	$ 31,629	$ 28,451

The tax effects of significant items comprising the Company's net deferred tax asset and liability as of December 31, 1993 are as follows (in thousands):

Current deferred tax asset:	
Accrued vacation	$ 2,634
Other accrued liabilities	4,742
Other	(682)
Total	6,694
Noncurrent deferred tax liability:	
Difference between book and tax basis of property	(13,976)
Other liabilities	5,542
Postretirement benefit obligation	2,085
Other	(44)
Total	(6,393)
Valuation allowance	0
Net deferred tax asset	$ 301

A reconciliation between the Federal income tax statutory rate and the Company's effective income tax rate is as follows:

	1993	1992	1991
Statutory rate	35.0%	34.0%	34.0%
State and local income taxes, net of Federal income tax benefit	5.0	4.3	4.0
Income from Puerto Rico	(3.7)	(3.3)	(2.3)
Other, net	2.4	0.8	1.8
Effective income tax rate	38.7%	35.8%	37.5%

9. SHAREHOLDERS' EQUITY: Each share of common stock includes a stock purchase right which is not currently exercisable but would become exercisable upon occurrence of certain events as provided for in the Rights Agreement. The rights expire on July 5, 1999.

10. EMPLOYEE STOCK PURCHASE PLAN: The Company has an Employee Stock Purchase Plan under which employees are granted an option to purchase shares of the Company's common stock during the quarter in which the option is granted. The option price is 85% of the fair market value of the stock at the beginning or end of the quarter, whichever is lower. Options for shares were exercised at prices ranging from $18.70 to $23.06 in 1993, $17.64 to $20.24 in 1992 and $16.26 to $19.60 in 1991. At December 31, 1993, there were 672,657 shares of common stock reserved for purchase under the plan.

11. STOCK OPTION PLANS: The Company has granted incentive and non-qualified stock options to certain key employees to purchase shares of the Company's common stock at the fair market value of the common stock on the date of the grant. The options generally become exercisable one year from the date of grant.

Option transactions during the three years ended December 31, 1993 are as follows:

	Shares	Exercise Price
Balance, Dec. 31, 1990	460,541	$ 9.11-25.13
Options		
Granted	68,000	22.75
Exercised	(76,202)	9.11-21.88
Cancelled	(47,100)	21.88-25.13
Balance, Dec. 31, 1991	405,239	9.11-25.13
Options		
Granted	92,500	23.88-24.75
Exercised	(90,414)	9.11-23.50
Cancelled	(47,176)	11.59-25.13
Balance, Dec. 31, 1992	360,149	9.11-24.75
Options		
Granted	102,157	23.88-26.25
Exercised	(55,467)	9.11-23.50
Cancelled	(31,151)	11.34-24.75
Balance, Dec. 31, 1993	375,688	9.11-26.25

At December 31, 1993, there were options for 273,531 shares exercisable and 682,978 shares of common stock reserved for options under the plans.

12. PROFIT SHARING AND DEFERRED COMPENSATION: The Company has a non-contributory profit sharing plan to provide retirement income for most of its employees. The Company is required to contribute to the profit sharing plan's trust fund an amount equal to 7.5% of its income before income taxes and profit sharing contribution plus such additional amount as the Board of Directors may determine, up to a maximum of 15% of the aggregate compensation of participating employees (see Consolidated Statements of Income).

The Company has deferred compensation agreements with certain officers. The present value of cash benefits payable under the agreements is being provided over the periods of active employment. The charge to expense for the agreements was $345,000 in 1993, $286,000 in 1992 and $463,000 in 1991.

13. POSTRETIREMENT BENEFITS: The Company sponsors two defined postretirement benefit plans that cover qualifying salaried and non-salaried employees. One plan provides health care benefits and the other provides life insurance benefits. The medical plan is contributory and contributions are adjusted annually based on actual claims experience, while the life insurance plan is noncontributory. The Company's intent is that the retiree provide approximately 50% of the actual cost of providing the medical plan. Neither plan is funded.

In 1991, the Company adopted the provisions of SFAS No. 106, "Employers' Accounting for Postretirement Benefits Other Than Pensions" and elected immediate recognition of the transition amount of $3,816,000 ($2,385,000 after income taxes).

As of December 31, 1993, the accumulated postretirement benefit obligation ("APBO") was $7,614,000. The following table reconciles the plans status to the accrued postretirement health care and life insurance liability as reflected on the balance sheet as of December 31, (in thousands):

	1993	1992
APBO:		
Retirees	$ 1,890	$ 1,834
Fully eligible participants	1,790	1,057
Other participants	3,934	2,907
	7,614	5,798
Unrecognized net loss	(1,195)	(457)
Accrued postretirement benefit obligation included in Other Liabilities	$ 6,419	$ 5,341

Net postretirement costs are summarized as follows (in thousands):

	1993	1992	1991
Service costs	$ 245	$ 184	$ 131
Interest on APBO	523	456	338
Net periodic postretirement cost	$ 768	$ 640	$ 469

For measurement purposes, the cost of providing medical benefits was assumed to increase by 12% in 1993, decreasing to an annual rate of 7.5% after 1998. The medical cost trend rate assumption could have a significant effect on amounts reported. An increase of 1% in the assumed rate of

(continued)

increase would have had the effect of increasing the APBO by $851,000 and the net periodic postretirement cost by $113,000. The weighted average discount rate used in determining the APBO was 7.5% in 1993, 8.5% in 1992 and 9% in 1991 and employee earnings were estimated to increase 4.5% annually until age 65.

14. FINANCIAL INSTRUMENTS: The following methods and assumptions were used to estimate the fair value of each class of financial instruments for which it is practicable to estimate that value:

Short-term investments - The carrying amount approximates fair value because of the short maturity of those instruments.

Long-term investments - The fair values of certain investments are estimated based on quoted market prices. The fair values of the Company's investments in limited partnerships are based on estimates by general partners in the absence of readily ascertainable market values. For the Company's other investments, which are not actively traded and are immaterial, fair value is based on an estimate of the net realizable value of those investments.

Long-term debt - The fair values of the Company's convertible debentures are based on recent market quotes. The fair value of the other long-term debt is based on estimated rates currently available to the Company for debt with similar terms and maturities.

The carrying value and estimated fair values of the Company's financial instruments at December 31, 1993 and 1992 are as follows (in thousands):

	Carrying Value		Fair Value	
	1993	1992	1993	1992
Assets:				
Short-term investments	$ 1,900	$ 150	$ 1,900	$ 150
Long-term investments	8,103	7,705	9,169	8,601
Liabilities:				
Long-term debt	111,542	12,622	112,105	13,931

15. COMMITMENTS AND CONTINGENCIES: Total rental expense was $12,257,000 in 1993, $6,969,000 in 1992, and $3,731,000 in 1991. Minimum annual rentals under non-cancellable operating leases total $22,471,000 and range from $7,536,000 in 1994 to $1,847,000 in 1998.

16. SUBSEQUENT EVENT: On January 7, 1994, the Company acquired Marketing Profiles, Inc. ("MPI") for $18,000,000 in cash and a contingent purchase payment payable in 1997 to the former MPI shareholders. The contingent purchase payment is based upon a multiple of MPI's 1996 operating results as defined in the acquisition agreement. The acquisition price was funded with a portion of the proceeds received in the December 1993 issuance of long-term debt (See Note 7). The acquisition will be accounted for using the purchase method of accounting and, accordingly, the results of operations of MPI will be included in the Company's consolidated financial statements from the date of acquisition. MPI is based in Maitland, Florida and is a database marketing and consulting company which provides software products and related marketing services to the financial industry.

INDEPENDENT AUDITORS' REPORT

To the Board of Directors and Shareholders,
John H. Harland Company:

We have audited the accompanying consolidated balance sheets of John H. Harland Company and its subsidiaries as of December 31, 1993 and 1992, and the related consolidated statements of income, cash flows and shareholders' equity for each of the three years in the period ended December 31, 1993. These financial statements are the responsibility of the Company's management. Our responsibility is to express an opinion on these financial statements based on our audits.

We conducted our audits in accordance with generally accepted auditing standards. Those standards require that we plan and perform the audit to obtain reasonable assurance about whether the financial statements are free of material misstatement. An audit includes examining, on a test basis, evidence supporting the amounts and disclosures in the financial statements. An audit also includes assessing the accounting principles used and significant estimates made by management, as well as evaluating the overall financial statement presentation. We believe that our audits provide a reasonable basis for our opinion.

In our opinion, the consolidated financial statements referred to above present fairly, in all material respects, the financial position of John H. Harland Company and its subsidiaries as of December 31, 1993 and 1992, and the results of their operations and their cash flows for each of the three years in the period ended December 31, 1993, in conformity with generally accepted accounting principles.

As discussed in Note 8 to the consolidated financial statements, effective January 1, 1993, the Company changed its method of accounting for income taxes to conform with the provisions of Statement of Financial Accounting Standards No. 109.

Deloitte & Touche

DELOITTE & TOUCHE

Atlanta, Georgia
January 28, 1994

MANAGEMENT RESPONSIBILITY FOR FINANCIAL STATEMENTS

The financial statements included in this report were prepared by the Company in conformity with generally accepted accounting principles consistently applied. Management's best estimates and judgments were used, where appropriate. Management is responsible for the integrity of the financial statements and for other financial information included in this report. The financial statements have been audited by the Company's independent auditors, Deloitte & Touche. As set forth in their report, their audits were conducted in accordance with generally accepted auditing standards and formed the basis for their opinion on the accompanying financial statements. They consider the Company's control structure and perform such tests and other procedures as they deem necessary to express an opinion on the fairness of the financial statements.

The Company maintains a control structure which is designed to provide reasonable assurance that assets are safeguarded and that the financial records reflect the authorized transactions of the Company. As a part of this process, the Company has an internal audit function which evaluates the adequacy and effectiveness of the control structure.

The Audit Committee of the Board of Directors includes directors who are neither officers nor employees of the Company. The Committee meets periodically with management, internal auditors and the independent auditors to discuss auditing, the Company's control structure and financial reporting matters. The Director of Internal Audit and the independent auditors have full and free access to meet with the Audit Committee.

William M. Dollar

William M. Dollar
Vice President, Treasurer and
Chief Financial Officer

SELECTED QUARTERLY FINANCIAL DATA, DIVIDENDS PAID AND STOCK PRICE RANGE

(IN THOUSANDS EXCEPT PER SHARE AMOUNTS)	Quarter Ended			
	March 31	June 30	September 30	December 31
1993				
Net sales	$ 133,504	$ 129,979	$ 129,922	$ 126,081
Gross profit	58,928	59,814	56,892	55,066
Net income	13,119	14,127	13,318	11,958
Per common share:				
Net income	.39	.42	.42	.39
Dividends paid	.235	.235	.235	.235
Stock market price:				
High	27 1/2	28 1/8	27 3/4	25 5/8
Low	24 1/4	25 5/8	25 1/4	20 7/8
1992				
Net sales	$ 103,629	$ 113,766	$ 113,975	$ 113,610
Gross profit	49,917	53,677	52,804	52,023
Net income	14,869	14,530	13,671	13,568
Per common share:				
Net income	.41	.40	.39	.39
Dividends paid	.225	.225	.225	.225
Stock market price:				
High	25 1/4	25	24 1/4	27 1/4
Low	22 1/8	20 1/2	20 5/8	22 1/2

The Company's common stock (symbol: JH) is listed on the New York Stock Exchange..At December 31, 1993 there were 8,044 shareholders of record.

SELECTED FINANCIAL DATA

(IN THOUSANDS EXCEPT PER SHARE AMOUNTS)	1993	1992	1991	1990	1989
Net sales	$ 519,486	$ 444,980	$ 378,659	$ 366,834	$ 344,734
Net income	52,522	56,638	47,435	57,167	58,052
Total assets	356,451	339,880	351,554	347,105	321,081
Long-term debt	111,542	12,622	11,661	11,304	11,276
Per common share:					
Net income	1.62	1.59	1.27	1.52	1.54
Cash dividends	94	.90	.86	.78	.68
Average number of shares					
outstanding	32,460	35,689	37,469	37,604	37,797

Refer to Note 13 on page 26 regarding the impact of change in accounting method for postretirement benefits in 1991 and to Note 4 on page 24 for impact of a restructuring charge in 1991. Refer to Note 3 on page 23 regarding the impact of acquisitions in 1992 and 1993.

Management's Discussion And Analysis
Of Results Of Operations and Financial Conditions

The following comments should be read in conjunction with the President's letter to shareholders on pages 2 to 4 and the consolidated financial statements and notes thereto on pages 18 to 27.

Results Of Operations
1993 versus 1992

1993 consolidated net sales increased $74.5 million or 16.7% over 1992 and represented the 44th consecutive year of sales increases. The Company's Financial Services Group ("FSG") had a net sales increase of $72.1 million or 18.4% which consisted of an 18.1% increase in units and a price and product mix increase of 0.3%. The FSG sales increase is attributable to the acquisition of Rocky Mountain Bank Note Company ("RMBN") in January 1993 coupled with the impact of the February 1992 acquisition of Interchecks, Inc. ("Interchecks") (see Note 3 on page 23). Competitive pricing pressures within the check printing industry contributed to the mild change in the FSG price and product mix. Net sales by the Company's Data Services Group ("DSG") increased $2.4 million or 4.6% in 1993 primarily due to increases in hardware sales and service-related revenues while 1993 form sales were flat compared to 1992. The hardware sales and service-related revenue increases offset sales decreases by DSG's European sales subsidiary Datascan and the loss of revenues associated with American Testronics Company, the assets of which were sold in June 1992.

Consolidated cost of goods sold increased $52.2 million or 22.1% and increased as a percentage of sales to 55.6% from 53.2% in 1992. FSG's cost of goods sold increased as a percentage of sales to 56.0% from 53.4% in 1992 primarily due to acquired operations, which had lower margins, and duplication of costs during integration of acquired operations. FSG achieved labor productivity improvements of 0.6% in 1993. DSG's cost of goods sold increased slightly as a percentage of sales to 51.8% in 1993 from 51.1% in 1992. DSG's gross margin improved as a result of the 1992 sale of American Testronics Company, which had lower margins, but the improvement was offset by increased machine sales and service-related revenues, which have lower margins than forms, and by increased product development costs.

Consolidated selling, general and administrative expenses increased $14.0 million or 12.6% in 1993 primarily due to acquired operations, higher information systems costs and increases in employee health care costs. As a percentage of sales, consolidated selling, general and administrative expenses decreased from 25.0% in 1992 to 24.1% in 1993. The consolidation of selling and certain administrative functions of the acquired operations was a primary factor contributing to this decrease. Profit sharing costs increased $0.5 million but decreased as a percentage of sales from 2.0% in 1992 to 1.9% in 1993.

Due to the February 1992 acquisition of Interchecks and the January 1993 acquisition of RMBN, amortization of intangibles increased $4.0 million over 1992 and was 1.7% as a percentage of sales in 1993 compared to 1.1% in 1992. Of the total 1993 amortization of intangibles, $8.0 million relates to intangible assets which are being amortized over 5 years.

Interest and other income (expense) - net decreased $6.4 million from 1992. The primary components of the change were gains of $3.4 million realized in 1992 on the dispositions of American Testronics Company and the Puerto Rico bond investment portfolio and increased interest expense, which totaled $2.6 million in 1993 due to increased levels of debt. Another component of the interest and other income (expense) net change was reduced interest income earned in 1993 due to lower average cash and investment balances.

Income before income taxes decreased $2.6 million or 2.9% from 1992 and decreased as a percentage of sales from 19.8% in 1992 to 16.5% in 1993. The effective consolidated income tax rate for 1993 was 38.7% compared to 35.8% in 1992. The effective tax rate increased primarily as a result of the Omnibus Tax Reconciliation Act of 1993, which increased the federal corporate tax rate from 34% to 35%, and certain nonrecurring tax exempt items and higher tax exempt income in 1992.

1992 VERSUS 1991

Consolidated 1992 sales increased $66.3 million or 17.5% over 1991. Both FSG and DSG experienced sales increases with FSG contributing $60.7 million of the increase and DSG contributing $5.6 million. FSG's sales growth was attributable to a 25.7% increase in check unit production tempered by a 7.4% reduction from price and product mix. The unit increase came principally from the new business obtained through the acquisition of Interchecks in February 1992 with a lesser portion due to an increase in FSG's core business. Lower pricing in 1992 resulted from competitive conditions in the check printing industry. DSG's sales increased 11.8% partially due to the consolidation of Datascan's results of operations after acquisition of the remaining 50% of Datascan's stock in December 1991 and to sales increases in educational markets.

Consolidated gross profit margin declined in 1992 to 46.8% from 49.9% in 1991. Margins in both FSG and DSG were negatively impacted by acquired operations (Interchecks and Datascan, respectively); however, FSG realized an increase in labor efficiency of 3.6% in its core operations as a result of completion of the conversion to offset printing and computerized production systems in 1991. DSG's margin declines were moderated by the sales increase in standard forms in its educational markets which generally provide higher margins.

Selling, general and administrative expenses increased $17.0 million in 1992 or 18.1% and, as a percentage of sales, increased to 25.0% from 24.8% in 1991. The primary components of this increase were employee health care costs, the costs of enhanced data processing systems, expenses of acquired operations and marketing costs associated with customer relations. Profit sharing costs increased $1.0 million but decreased as a percentage of sales from 2.1% in 1991 to 2.0% in 1992.

Amortization of intangibles costs associated with the acquired operations totaled $4.7 million or 1.1% as a percentage of sales.

Interest and other income decreased $0.5 million or 9.5% from 1991, which is attributable to both lower interest rates and significantly lower investment balances, a result of the use of funds for the acquisitions of Interchecks and Datascan and for the stock repurchase program. The reduced interest and other income was offset by $3.4 million of gains realized in the sale of the Puerto Rico bond investment portfolio and the sale of the assets of American Testronics Company.

The Company's effective consolidated income tax rate decreased to 35.8% from 37.5% primarily due to the higher level of tax exempt income in 1992.

OUTLOOK

The Company will continue its efforts to further diversify its business during 1994. On January 7, 1994, the Company acquired Marketing Profiles, Inc. ("MPI"), a database marketing and consulting company which provides software products and related marketing services to the financial industry. See Note 16 on page 27.

In October 1993, the Company announced the formation of a new subsidiary, The Check Store, Inc. ("The Check Store"), which will market checks and related products directly to consumers. The direct marketing of checks and related products to consumers is currently the fastest growing segment of the check printing market and The Check Store, which will become operational during the first half of 1994, represents the Company's entry into this distribution channel. It is anticipated that The Check Store will have lower margins than the Company's traditional check printing operations and, due to start-up costs and expenditures for marketing and product development, will negatively impact the Company's results and cash flows during 1994. The Company is unable to determine if or when The Check Store operations will contribute positively to cash flow or operating results.

The Company expects that its check printing operations will continue to experience competitive pricing pressures during 1994, and as a result the price component of changes in revenue might be flat or negative. However, the Company anticipates that profit margins should experience a slight improvement in 1994 as a result of the continued integration of acquired operations along with other cost control measures.

FINANCIAL CONDITION, CAPITAL RESOURCES AND LIQUIDITY

Cash flows provided by operations in 1993 were $90.7 million compared to $78.4 million in 1992, an increase of 15.7%. The primary uses of funds in 1993 were for the purchase of the Company's common stock, the acquisition of the net assets of RMBN, additions to property, plant and equipment and dividends paid to the Company's shareholders.

In December 1993, the Company issued $85.0 million of Series A Senior Notes ("Senior Notes") with a final maturity of December 2008, and also arranged a $15.0 Million Term Loan ("Term Loan") due December 2003. The Senior Notes and the Term Loan have a fixed annual interest rate of 6.60% and 6.63%, respectively. Proceeds from these obligations were used to repay amounts outstanding under short-term lines of credit and to fund the January 1994 purchase of MPI and will be used to fund additional purchases of Company stock and for general corporate purposes.

The Company has unsecured lines of credit which provide for borrowing up to $111.0 million. At December 31, 1993, no amounts were outstanding under these lines, a decrease of $18.0 million from December 31, 1992.

Excluding the borrowings under the unsecured lines of credit, which the Company replaced with long-term financing, the ratio of current assets to current liabilities increased from 2.7 at December 31, 1992 to 3.1 at December 31, 1993, and working capital increased to $90.9 million at December 31, 1993 from $69.2 million at December 31, 1992.

In March 1993, the Company completed a program announced in November 1991 to repurchase 4.0 million shares of its common stock. In June 1993, the Company initiated a new program to repurchase 3.4 million additional common shares which was completed in November 1993 at an average cost of $26.24 per share. In December 1993, the Company announced another program to repurchase 1.5 million common shares but had not purchased any shares under this program as of December 31, 1993.

Additions to property, plant and equipment for 1993 were $27.1 million compared to $18.7 million in 1992. The Company anticipates 1994 capital expenditures will total approximately $37 million.

On December 31, 1993, the Company had $28.1 million in cash and cash equivalents and short-term investments. The Company believes that its current cash position, funds from operations and available amounts under its lines of credit will be sufficient to meet anticipated requirements for working capital, dividends, capital expenditures, the purchase of MPI, the announced stock repurchase program and other corporate needs.

SENIOR CORPORATE OFFICERS

ROBERT R. WOODSON
Chairman, President
& Chief Executive Officer

I. WARD LANG
Vice Chairman, General
Counsel & Secretary

WILLIAM M. DOLLAR
Vice President, Treasurer
& Chief Financial Officer

SAM D. HARRISON
Senior Vice President

EARL W. ROGERS JR.
Senior Vice President

MICHAEL S. RUPE
Senior Vice President

DONALD K. VOSHALL
Senior Vice President

OTHER CORPORATE / STAFF OFFICERS

S. ARLENE BATES
Vice President

WILLIAM A. THURBER
Assistant Treasurer

VICTORIA P. WEYAND
Vice President & Assistant Secretary

FINANCIAL SERVICES SENIOR OFFICERS

Vice Presidents
RALPH W. BRICKER JR.
ROBERT N. GLEZEN
CECELIA B. MORKEN
DON R. STUCKEY

SUBSIDIARY OFFICERS

THOMAS R. HOAG
President & Chief Executive Officer,
Scantron Corporation

DIVIDENDS & MAILINGS

Dividends:
Cash dividends on Harland common stock are normally paid in the months of March, June, September and December.

Dividend Reinvestment:
Through Harland's Automatic Dividend Reinvestment Plan shareholders may automatically reinvest cash dividends to acquire additional shares of Harland common stock. The plan provides a simple and convenient method of acquiring additional shares of Harland common stock in a manner which affords savings in commissions for most shareholders. For additional information regarding the Dividend Reinvestment Plan contact our Transfer Agent at:

Trust Company Bank
Corporate Trust Department
P.O. Box 4625
Atlanta, Georgia 30302
800-568-3476

Mailings:
Beginning first quarter 1994, John H. Harland Company will discontinue its practice of automatically mailing quarterly reports to shareholders whose shares are registered in the name of a bank, broker or nominee. Any shareholder wishing to receive copies of the Company's quarterly reports may send a written request to the Corporate Office, Investor Relations Department.

Duplicate mailings may occur when more than one person in the same household owns stock or an individual holds stock in more than one name. The Company is required to mail information to each name on the shareholder list, unless a shareholder requests that duplicate mailings be eliminated. Requests to eliminate duplicate mailings should be sent in writing to the Transfer Agent and should indicate specific name(s) to be kept on the list and name(s) to delete.

10-K Report:
John H. Harland Company's annual report on Form 10-K, together with the financial statements and the notes thereto, is filed with the Securities and Exchange Commission. Copies may be obtained by writing to the Corporate Office, Investor Relations Department.

The Limited, Inc.

Financial Summary

(thousands except per share amounts, ratios and store and associate data)

Fiscal Year	1993**	1992	1991*	1990*
Summary of Operations				
Net Sales	$7,245,088	$6,944,296	$6,149,218	$5,253,509
Gross Income	1,958,835	1,990,740	1,793,543	1,630,439
Operating Income	701,556	788,698	712,700	697,537
Income Before Income Taxes	644,999	745,497	660,302	653,438
Net Income	$390,999	$455,497	$403,302	$398,438
Net Income as a Percentage of Sales	5.4%	6.6%	6.6%	7.6%
Per Share Results				
Net Income	$1.08	$1.25	$1.11	$1.10
Dividends	$.36	$.28	$.28	$.24
Book Value	$6.82	$6.25	$5.19	$4.33
Weighted Average Shares Outstanding	363,234	363,738	363,594	362,044
Other Financial Information				
Total Assets	$4,135,105	$3,846,450	$3,418,856	$2,871,878
Working Capital	$1,513,181	$1,063,352	$1,084,205	$884,004
Current Ratio	3.1	2.5	3.1	2.8
Long-Term Debt	$650,000	$541,639	$713,758	$540,446
Debt-to-Equity Ratio	27%	24%	38%	35%
Shareholders' Equity	$2,441,293	$2,267,617	$1,876,792	$1,560,052
Return on Average Shareholders' Equity	17%	22%	23%	28%
Stores and Associates at End of Year				
Total Number of Stores Open	4,623	4,425	4,194	3,760
Selling Square Feet	24,426,000	22,863,000	20,355,000	17,008,000
Number of Associates	97,500	100,700	83,800	72,500

† Fifty-three week fiscal year.

* Includes the results of companies acquired subsequent to the date of acquisition.

** Includes the results of companies disposed of up to the disposition date.

CONTROLLED INVENTORIES AND EXPENSES, IS A MUST

1989†**	1988*	1987	1986	1985*	1984†	1983
$4,647,916	$4,070,777	$3,527,941	$3,142,696	$2,387,110	$1,343,134	$1,085,890
1,446,635	1,214,703	992,775	961,827	718,843	404,321	327,616
625,254	467,418	408,872	438,229	276,212	173,102	135,377
573,926	396,136	378,188	394,780	239,317	157,495	134,939
$346,926	$245,136	$235,188	$227,780	$145,317	$92,495	$70,939
7.5%	6.0%	6.7%	7.2%	6.1%	6.9%	6.5%
$.96	$.68	$.62	$.60	$.40	$.26	$.20
$.16	$.12	$.12	$.08	$.05	$.04	$.02
$3.45	$2.64	$2.04	$2.07	$1.13	$.77	$.54
361,288	360,186	376,626	376,860	365,638	361,262	360,372
$2,418,486	$2,145,506	$1,929,477	$1,726,544	$1,494,313	$657,242	$425,240
$685,524	$567,639	$629,783	$586,827	$419,706	$180,960	$101,665
2.4	2.2	2.9	2.7	2.2	2.0	1.8
$445,674	$517,952	$681,000	$417,420	$670,744	$150,139	$68,763
36%	55%	93%	53%	166%	55%	36%
$1,240,454	$946,207	$729,171	$781,542	$404,075	$275,403	$192,576
32%	29%	31%	38%	43%	40%	45%
3,344	3,497	3,115	2,682	2,353	1,412	937
14,374,000	14,296,000	12,795,000	11,320,000	10,460,000	5,166,000	3,667,000
63,000	56,700	50,200	43,200	33,600	17,700	15,300

Management's Discussion and Analysis

Results of Operations

Net sales for the fourth quarter grew to $2.421 billion, an increase of 4% from $2.319 billion a year ago (excluding Brylane sales in each period). Net income was $196 million, compared to $244 million last year, and earnings per share were $0.54 versus $0.67 in 1992.

Net sales for the 52-week fiscal year ended January 29, 1994 were $7.245 billion, an increase in excess of $500 million from sales of $6.733 billion last year (excluding Brylane sales in each comparable period). Net income was $391 million compared to $455 million a year ago. Earnings per share were $1.08 compared to $1.25 last year.

The women's apparel businesses (Express, Limited Stores, Lerner, Lane Bryant and Henri Bendel) had a disappointing year, as their total sales were flat for the year, comparable store sales declined 5% and operating income declined in the fourth quarter and full year (with the exception of Henri Bendel for the full year).

In contrast, for the Company's non-women's apparel businesses (Victoria's Secret Stores, Victoria's Secret Catalogue, Structure, The Limited Too, Abercrombie & Fitch Co., Bath & Body Works, Cacique and Penhaligon's), 1993 was a particularly successful year as they increased their total sales by 27% and contributed in excess of 40% of the Company's pre-tax earnings.

Divisional highlights include the following:
- Victoria's Secret Stores delivered the highest operating income dollars in the Company and the best in their history.
- Victoria's Secret Catalogue produced the best fourth quarter and full year operating income in their history.
- Bath & Body Works had record profitability in the fourth quarter, and the year's largest increase in comparable store sales and operating income rate of the Company's businesses.
- The Limited Too more than doubled their profitability and had record comparable store sales in the fourth quarter, and delivered record comparable store sales and their first ever profit for the full year.
- Abercrombie & Fitch Co. more than doubled their profitability in the fourth quarter, and also delivered their first ever profit for the full year.

Financial Summary

The following summarized financial data compares 1993 to the comparable periods for 1992 and 1991:

(Sales in millions)	1993	1992	1991	% Change 1993-92	% Change 1992-91
Retail Sales	$6,567	$6,153	$5,388	7%	14%
Catalogue Sales	678	791	761	(14%)	4%
Total Net Sales	$7,245	$6,944	$6,149	4%	13%
Increase (Decrease) in Comparable Store Sales	(1%)	2%	3%		
Retail Sales Increase Attributable to New and Remodeled Stores	8%	12%	14%		
Retail Sales per Average Selling Square Foot	$278	$285	$288	(2%)	(1%)
Retail Sales per Average Store (thousands)	$1,452	$1,428	$1,355	2%	5%
Average Store Size at End of Year (square feet)	5,284	5,167	4,853	2%	6%
Retail Selling Square Feet (thousands)	24,426	22,863	20,355	7%	12%
Number of Stores: Beginning of Year	4,425	4,194	3,760		
Opened	322	323	484		
Closed	(124)	(92)	(50)		
End of Year	4,623	4,425	4,194		

OUR NON-WOMEN'S APPAREL BUSINESSES HAVE THE POTEN

Net Sales

Fourth quarter 1993 sales of $2.421 billion were flat to last year due primarily to the sale of a 60% interest in the Brylane division on August 30, 1993. Excluding Brylane sales from last year, fourth quarter sales would have increased 4% due to an 8% increase in sales attributable to new and remodeled stores. Fourth quarter 1992 sales increased 18% primarily due to the productivity of comparable stores which increased 8%, combined with the 9% increase in sales attributed to new and remodeled stores.

The 1993 retail sales increase is attributable to the net addition of new and remodeled stores. The Company added 322 new stores in 1993, remodeled 239 stores and closed 124 stores for a net addition of 198 stores and in excess of 1.5 million square feet of new retail selling space. However, average sales productivity declined slightly to $278 per square foot.

Catalogue sales decreased 14% in 1993, reflecting the sale of Brylane and the resulting elimination of their sales in the third and fourth quarters. Had last year's catalogue sales excluded Brylane, catalogue sales would have increased 19% as the number of books mailed during the year increased while the average demand per book decreased slightly.

In 1992, retail sales increased as a result of the 2% increase in comparable store sales combined with the net addition of 231 stores and approximately 2.5 million selling square feet. Average store size in 1992 increased 6% to 5,167 square feet, while sales per average store increased 5%, resulting in a slight decline in average sales productivity to $285 per square foot.

Catalogue sales increased 4% in 1992, reflecting a 3% increase in the number of books mailed, and a slight increase in customer demand per book.

Gross Income

Gross income decreased as a percentage of sales to 29.1% for the fourth quarter of 1993 from 32.2% for the same period in 1992. Merchandise margins, expressed as a percentage of sales, decreased 1.4% reflecting a higher level of promotional activity (particularly in the women's apparel businesses) to liquidate seasonal inventories. In addition, buying and occupancy costs as a percentage of sales, increased 1.6% primarily as a result of lower sales productivity associated with several of the Company's women's apparel businesses.

The fourth quarter 1992 gross income rate of 32.2% was flat when compared to 1991. Buying and occupancy costs, expressed as a percentage of sales, declined 1.0%, reflecting the favorable leveraging of these largely fixed costs by the 8% gain in comparable store sales. Merchandise margins, expressed as a percentage of sales, decreased by approximately the same amount, reflecting a generally higher level of promotional activity.

The 1993 gross income rate of 27.0% was 1.7% below the rate for 1992. Merchandise margins, expressed as a percentage of sales, decreased .4% reflecting higher promotional activity, notably in the fourth quarter. Buying and occupancy costs were not sufficiently leveraged (particularly at the Company's women's apparel businesses) and as a result, these costs increased approximately 1.2%, expressed as a percentage of sales.

The 1992 gross income rate of 28.7% was 0.5% below the rate for 1991. Buying and occupancy costs, as a percentage of sales, increased 0.5% during the year principally as a result of lower sales productivity associated with new and remodeled stores. Selling productivity, expressed in terms of sales per average selling square foot, is typically lower in new and remodeled stores during the initial years of operation because these stores are typically larger than average existing stores. Merchandise margins were about flat compared to the prior year.

General, Administrative and Store Operating Expenses

General, administrative and store operating expenses, expressed as a percentage of sales, were 15.1% in both the fourth quarter of 1993 and 1992. Management continues to emphasize selling payroll management and expense control.

These costs, expressed as a percentage of sales, were 17.4%, 17.3% and 17.6% for fiscal years 1993, 1992 and 1991. The major component of these costs is store payroll which for the last three years has increased at a comparable or lower rate than sales for the respective period. The Company anticipates this trend will continue in fiscal year 1994.

Special and Nonrecurring Items

During 1993, management approved a restructuring plan which focused on the enhancement of core retail operations and the utilization of underperforming retail assets of the businesses. The specifics of the plan, as described more fully in Note 2 to the consolidated financial statements,

TIAL TO BE MORE PROFITABLE THAN THE WOMEN'S DIVISIONS.

included the following: the sale of a 60% interest in the Brylane mail order business; the acceleration of the store remodeling, downsizing and closing program at the Limited Stores and Lerner divisions; and the refocusing of the merchandise strategy at the Henri Bendel division.

The 60% sale of Brylane allows management to increase their focus on growing core retail operations as well as to improve the operations at underperforming divisions. In an effort to improve the performance of the Company's Limited Stores and Lerner divisions, management developed an action plan that focused on underperforming store assets, with the objective of properly sizing these stores and remodeling them in an up-to-date format by the end of 1995. In addition, the plan also included the closing of approximately 100 underperforming stores (primarily in the Lerner and Limited Stores retail businesses) and a writedown of underperforming assets to net realizable value.

The net impact of the restructuring plan, including the sale of the Company's interest in Brylane, is anticipated to be immaterial to future operations. The Company's reduced share of Brylane's operating income is expected to be offset by improved sales productivity and reduced depreciation and amortization costs resulting from the restructuring.

The Company also announced a program to repurchase up to $500 million of the Company's common stock over time as market conditions warrant. As of the end of the year, the Company had repurchased 5,287,600 shares at a cost of $93.3 million. Market conditions will dictate any future purchases.

Interest Expense

| | Fourth Quarter | | Year-to-Date | | |
	1993	1992	1993	1992	1991
Average Daily Borrowings (in millions)	$848.2	$993.7	$822.5	$1,046.3	$877.4
Average Effective Interest Rate	7.62%	6.07%	7.76%	5.96%	7.29%

Interest expense increased slightly in the fourth quarter and for all 1993 as compared to the comparable periods in 1992. Higher interest rates increased costs approximately $3.3 million and $14.8 million respectively during the fourth quarter and all of 1993. The average effective interest rate increased primarily due to the Company's decision to capitalize on favorable long-term interest rates by issuing $250 million principal amount of 7½% Debentures on March 15, 1993. The effective interest rate increase was offset by lower borrowing levels during the fourth quarter and all of 1993 which resulted in lower interest costs of approximately $2.2 million and $13.3 million, respectively.

Operating Income
Operating income, as a percentage of sales, was 9.6%, 11.4% and 11.6% for fiscal years 1993, 1992 and 1991. The decrease in 1993 was principally due to the 1.7% decline in gross income rate as discussed in more detail above.

Gain on Issuance of United Retail Group, Inc. Stock
The 1992 results include a $9 million pre-tax gain which resulted from the March, 1992 initial public offering of United Retail Group, Inc. (URGI), a specialty retailer of large-size woman's apparel. URGI sold approximately 3.7 million shares of common stock at $15 per share and received total consideration of approximately $55.6 million. Prior to the initial public offering, the Company owned approximately a 33% equity interest; subsequent to the initial public offering, the Company's ownership was diluted to approximately 20%. See Note 1 to the consolidated financial statements for further discussion of this matter.

Acquisitions
Gryphon Development, L.P. (Gryphon) creates, develops and manufactures most of the bath and personal care products sold by the Company. Prior to June 1, 1991, the Company owned approximately 50% of Gryphon and accounted for such investment using the equity method. Effective June 1, 1991, the Company acquired an additional 15% of Gryphon for $18.75 million and began including Gryphon in its consolidated financial statements.

Effective April 10, 1992, the Company acquired the remaining 35% of Gryphon for approximately $60 million and separately entered into a non-compete agreement with certain of the former Gryphon partners in return for warrants to purchase 1.5 million shares of the Company's common stock. This acquisition had no material effect on the Company's results of operations or financial condition.

EARNING 10% AFTER-TAXES WILL BE ACHIEVED BY GROWING

Management's Discussion and Analysis

Financial Condition

The Company's balance sheet at January 29, 1994 provides continuing evidence of financial strength and flexibility. The Company's debt-to-equity ratio was only 27% at the end of 1993 and the current ratio exceeded 3.1. A more detailed discussion of liquidity, capital resources and capital expenditures follows:

Liquidity and Capital Resources

Cash provided from operating activities, commercial paper backed by funds available under committed long-term credit agreements and the Company's capital structure continue to provide the resources to support operations, including projected growth, seasonal requirements and capital expenditures. A summary of the Company's working capital position and capitalization follows:

(thousands)	1993	1992	1991
Cash provided by operating activities	$448,139	$754,128	$475,637
Working capital	$1,513,181	$1,063,352	$1,084,205
Capitalization: Long-term debt	$650,000	$541,639	$713,758
Deferred income taxes	275,101	274,844	267,315
Shareholders' equity	2,441,293	2,267,617	1,876,792
Total capitalization	$3,366,394	$3,084,100	$2,857,865
Additional amounts available under long-term credit agreements	$840,000	$811,000	$536,000

The Company considers the following to be several measures of liquidity and capital resources:

	1993	1992	1991
Debt-to-equity ratio (long-term debt divided by shareholders' equity)	27%	24%	38%
Debt-to-capitalization ratio (long-term debt divided by total capitalization)	19%	18%	25%
Interest coverage ratio (income before interest expense, depreciation, amortization and income taxes divided by interest expense)	15x	17x	15x
Cash flow to capital investment (net cash provided by operating activities divided by capital expenditures)	151%	176%	91%

Net cash provided by operating activities totalled $448.1 million, $754.1 million and $475.6 million for 1993, 1992 and 1991 and continues to serve as the Company's primary source of liquidity. During 1993 and 1992, cash provided by operating activities and the proceeds from the sale of a 60% interest in the Brylane division exceeded cash requirements for capital additions, business acquisitions and dividend payments.

Depreciation and amortization have increased as a result of the Company's continued investment in new and remodeled stores. Cash requirements for accounts receivable grew from the introduction of proprietary credit cards at the Limited Stores, Structure and Victoria's Secret Catalogue divisions during 1993. Cash requirements for inventories and accounts payable and accrued expenses have varied during the three year period based on sales volumes.

Investing activities included capital expenditures, primarily new and remodeled stores, the sale of 60% of the Company's interest in Brylane, reduced by income taxes on the gain on sale, and the two-step acquisition of Gryphon.

Financing activities included $93.3 million of common stock the Company repurchased in the fourth quarter, representing approximately 5.3 million shares. Cash dividends paid by the Company in 1993 increased 29% over cash dividends paid in both 1992 and 1991.

At January 29, 1994, the Company had available $840 million under their long-term credit agreements. In addition, the Company currently has the ability to offer up to $250 million of debt securities and warrants to purchase debt securities under a shelf registration

ALL OF OUR BUSINESSES TO THEIR POTENTIAL

statement after giving effect to the sale by the Company, in March 1993, of $250 million 7½% Debentures due 2023.

Capital Expenditures

Capital expenditures amounted to $295.8 million, $429.5 million and $523.1 million for 1993, 1992 and 1991, respectively, of which $198.1 million, $258.2 million and $311.6 million were for new stores and remodeling and expanding existing stores. Approximately $29 million was expended in 1992 for the completion of the fulfillment center and office facility in Columbus, Ohio for Victoria's Secret Catalogue. In addition, office facilities previously committed under a long-term lease were acquired in 1992 for approximately $101 million.

The Company anticipates spending $375–$400 million for capital expenditures in 1994, of which $275–$300 million will be for new stores, the remodeling of existing stores and related improvements for the retail businesses. The Company expects that substantially all 1994 capital expenditures will be funded by net cash provided by operating activities.

The Company has announced its intention to add approximately 2.1 million selling square feet in 1994 which will result in a 9% increase over year-end 1993. It is anticipated the increase will result from the net addition of approximately 380 new stores and the remodeling of approximately 250 stores. A summary of stores and selling square feet by division for 1992 and 1993, and goals for 1994, follows:

	Goal-1994	1993	1992	Change From 1994-1993	Change From 1993-1992
Express					
Stores	751	673	640	78	33
Selling Sq. Ft.	4,746,000	3,902,000	3,470,000	844,000	432,000
Lerner New York					
Stores	848	877	915	(29)	(38)
Selling Sq. Ft.	6,542,000	6,802,000	6,963,000	(260,000)	(161,000)
The Limited					
Stores	716	746	759	(30)	(13)
Selling Sq. Ft.	4,402,000	4,482,000	4,257,000	(80,000)	225,000
Victoria's Secret Stores					
Stores	610	570	545	40	25
Selling Sq. Ft.	2,676,000	2,346,000	2,029,000	330,000	317,000
Lane Bryant					
Stores	827	817	809	10	8
Selling Sq. Ft.	3,954,000	3,852,000	3,755,000	102,000	97,000
Structure					
Stores	499	394	330	105	64
Selling Sq. Ft.	1,942,000	1,409,000	1,076,000	533,000	333,000
The Limited Too					
Stores	234	184	185	50	(1)
Selling Sq. Ft.	747,000	566,000	567,000	181,000	(1,000)
Bath & Body Works					
Stores	319	194	121	125	73
Selling Sq. Ft.	496,000	248,000	132,000	248,000	116,000
Abercrombie & Fitch Co.					
Stores	72	49	40	23	9
Selling Sq. Ft.	581,000	405,000	332,000	176,000	73,000
Henri Bendel					
Stores	4	4	4	0	0
Selling Sq. Ft.	93,000	93,000	93,000	0	0
Cacique					
Stores	115	108	71	7	37
Selling Sq. Ft.	344,000	318,000	186,000	26,000	132,000
Penhaligon's					
Stores	7	7	6	0	1
Selling Sq. Ft.	3,000	3,000	3,000	0	0
Total Retail Divisions					
Stores	5,002	4,623	4,425	379	198
Selling Sq. Ft.	26,526,000	24,426,000	22,863,000	2,100,000	1,563,000

WE WILL MAINTAIN THE FINANCIAL STRENGTH NECESSARY

Impact of Inflation

The Company's results of operations and financial condition are presented based upon historical cost. While it is difficult to accurately measure the impact of inflation due to the imprecise nature of the estimates required, the Company believes that the effects of inflation, if any, on the results of operations and financial condition have been minor.

Accounting for Income Taxes

Effective January 31, 1993, the Company adopted Statement of Financial Accounting Standard (SFAS) 109, "Accounting for Income Taxes." No cumulative effect adjustment was required as the difference in deferred income taxes under SFAS 109 and APB Opinion 11 was immaterial. The impact of adoption on the current year was also immaterial.

On August 10, 1993, the Federal income tax rate was retroactively increased 1% to 35% for 1993. As a result, it is estimated that the Company's effective tax rate will increase to 40% from 39% in future periods. There was no material impact from adjusting tax liabilities as a result of this retroactive increase. The Company believes this increase will not have a significant impact on future earnings.

Adoption of Accounting Standards

SFAS 112, "Employer's Accounting for Postemployment Benefits," was issued by the Financial Accounting Standards Board (FASB) in January, 1993. The Statement essentially requires, beginning in 1994, use of the accrual method of accounting for postemployment benefits such as salary continuation, severance pay, supplemental unemployment and disability related benefits if certain conditions are met. The Company believes that this pronouncement will have no material impact on the Company's financial statements under its current benefit structure.

TO EMBRACE CHANGE AND GROW THE BUSINESS.

Consolidated Statements of Income

(thousands except per share amounts)

	1993	1992	1991
Net Sales	$7,245,088	$6,944,296	$6,149,218
Costs of Goods Sold, Occupancy and Buying Costs	(5,286,253)	(4,953,556)	(4,355,675)
Gross Income	1,958,835	1,990,740	1,793,543
General, Administrative and Store Operating Expenses	(1,259,896)	(1,202,042)	(1,080,843)
Special and Nonrecurring Items, net	2,617	–	–
Operating Income	701,556	788,698	712,700
Interest Expense	(63,865)	(62,398)	(63,927)
Other Income, net	7,308	10,080	11,529
Gain on Issuance of United Retail Group Stock	–	9,117	–
Income Before Income Taxes	644,999	745,497	660,302
Provision for Income Taxes	254,000	290,000	257,000
Net Income	$390,999	$455,497	$403,302
Net Income Per Share	$1.08	$1.25	$1.11

The accompanying Notes are an integral part of these Consolidated Financial Statements.

OUR CUSTOMERS HELP TAKE OUR BUSINESSES IN NEW DIR

Consolidated Balance Sheets

(thousands)

Assets	Jan. 29, 1994	Jan. 30, 1993
Current Assets		
Cash and Equivalents	$320,558	$41,235
Accounts Receivable	1,056,911	837,377
Inventories	733,700	803,707
Other	109,456	101,811
Total Current Assets	2,220,625	1,784,130
Property and Equipment, net	1,666,588	1,813,948
Other Assets	247,892	248,372
Total Assets	$4,135,105	$3,846,450
Liabilities and Shareholders' Equity		
Current Liabilities		
Accounts Payable	$250,363	$309,092
Accrued Expenses	347,892	274,220
Certificates of Deposit	15,700	–
Income Taxes	93,489	137,466
Total Current Liabilities	707,444	720,778
Long-Term Debt	650,000	541,639
Deferred Income Taxes	275,101	274,844
Other Long-Term Liabilities	61,267	41,572
Shareholders' Equity		
Common Stock	189,727	189,727
Paid-in Capital	128,906	127,776
Retained Earnings	2,397,112	2,136,794
	2,715,745	2,454,297
Less: Treasury Stock, at cost	(274,452)	(186,680)
Total Shareholders' Equity	2,441,293	2,267,617
Total Liabilities and Shareholders' Equity	$4,135,105	$3,846,450

The accompanying Notes are an integral part of these Consolidated Financial Statements.

ECTIONS–TO NEW AVENUES OF DELIVERING MERCHANDISE

Consolidated Statements of Shareholders' Equity

(thousands)

	Common Stock	
	Shares Outstanding	Par Value
Balance, February 2, 1991	**360,598**	**$189,727**
Net Income	–	–
Cash Dividends	–	–
Exercise of Stock Options & Other	1,188	–
Balance, February 1, 1992	**361,786**	**189,727**
Net Income	–	–
Cash Dividends	–	–
Exercise of Stock Options & Other	862	–
Warrants Issued for Acquisition	–	–
Balance, January 30, 1993	**362,648**	**189,727**
Net Income	–	–
Cash Dividends	–	–
Purchase of Treasury Stock	(5,288)	–
Exercise of Stock Options & Other	441	–
Balance, January 29, 1994	**357,801**	**$189,727**

The accompanying Notes are an integral part of these Consolidated Financial Statements.

AND SERVICE.

Paid-in Capital	Retained Earnings	Treasury Stock, at Cost	Total Shareholders' Equity
$99,237	$1,480,866	$(209,778)	$1,560,052
–	403,302	–	403,302
–	(101,141)	–	(101,141)
1,692	–	12,887	14,579
100,929	1,783,027	(196,891)	1,876,792
–	455,497	–	455,497
–	(101,730)	–	(101,730)
6,598	–	10,211	16,809
20,249	–	–	20,249
127,776	2,136,794	(186,680)	2,267,617
–	390,999	–	390,999
–	(130,681)	–	(130,681)
–	–	(93,328)	(93,328)
1,130	–	5,556	6,686
$128,906	$2,397,112	$(274,452)	$2,441,293

WE'VE CLEARLY LEARNED THAT TEAMWORK IS KEY TO

Consolidated Statements of Cash Flows

(thousands)

	1993	1992	1991
Cash Flows from Operating Activities			
Net Income	$390,999	$455,497	$403,302
Impact of Other Operating Activities on Cash Flows			
Depreciation and Amortization	271,353	246,977	222,695
Special and Nonrecurring Items	(2,617)	–	–
Change in Assets and Liabilities			
Accounts Receivable	(219,534)	(101,545)	(65,536)
Inventories	70,006	(73,657)	(144,884)
Accounts Payable and Accrued Expenses	14,943	118,289	8,792
Income Taxes	20,773	82,369	30,371
Other Assets and Liabilities	(97,784)	26,198	20,897
Net Cash Provided by Operating Activities	448,139	754,128	475,637
Investing Activities			
Capital Expenditures	(295,804)	(429,545)	(523,082)
Businesses Acquired	–	(60,043)	(18,750)
Proceeds from Sale of Business	285,000	–	–
Tax Effect of Gain on Sale of Business	(64,750)	–	–
Cash Used for Investing Activities	(75,554)	(489,588)	(541,832)
Financing Activities			
Net (Repayments) Proceeds of Commercial Paper Borrowings and Certificates of Deposit	(25,939)	(322,119)	223,312
Repayments of Long-Term Debt	(100,000)	–	(50,000)
Proceeds from Issuance of Unsecured Notes	250,000	150,000	–
Dividends Paid	(130,681)	(101,730)	(101,141)
Purchase of Treasury Stock	(93,328)	–	–
Stock Options and Other	6,686	16,809	14,579
Net Cash (Used) Provided by Financing Activities	(93,262)	(257,040)	86,750
Net Increase in Cash and Equivalents	279,323	7,500	20,555
Cash and Equivalents, Beginning of Year	41,235	33,735	13,180
Cash and Equivalents, End of Year	$320,558	$41,235	$33,735

The accompanying Notes are an integral part of these Consolidated Financial Statements.

RESPONDING TO THE MARKETPLACE.

Notes to Consolidated Financial Statements

(thousands except per share amounts)

1 Summary of Significant Accounting Policies

Principles of Consolidation

The consolidated financial statements include the accounts of The Limited, Inc. (the Company) and all significant subsidiaries which are more than 50 percent owned and controlled. All significant intercompany balances and transactions have been eliminated in consolidation.

Investments in other entities (including joint ventures), which are more than 20 percent owned, are accounted for on the equity method.

Fiscal Year

The Company's fiscal year ends on the Saturday closest to January 31. Fiscal years are designated in the financial statements and notes by the calendar year in which the fiscal year commences. The results for fiscal year 1993, 1992 and 1991 represent the 52-week periods ended January 29, 1994, January 30, 1993 and February 1, 1992.

Cash and Equivalents

Cash and equivalents include amounts on deposit with financial institutions and money market investments with original maturities of less than 90 days.

Inventories

Inventories are principally valued at the lower of average cost or market, on a first-in first-out basis, utilizing the retail method.

Property and Equipment

Depreciation and amortization of property and equipment are computed for financial reporting purposes on a straight-line basis, using service lives ranging principally from 10–30 years for buildings and improvements and 3–10 years for other property and equipment. The cost of assets sold or retired and the related accumulated depreciation or amortization are removed from the accounts with any resulting gain or loss included in net income. Maintenance and repairs are charged to expense as incurred. Major renewals and betterments which extend service lives are capitalized.

Goodwill Amortization

Goodwill represents the excess of the purchase price over the fair value of the net assets of acquired companies and is amortized on a straight-line basis principally over 30 years.

Interest Rate Swap Agreements

The difference between the amount of interest to be paid and the amount of interest to be received under interest rate swap agreements due to changing interest rates is charged or credited to interest expense over the life of the swap agreement. Gains and losses from the disposition of swap agreements are deferred and amortized over the term of the related agreements.

Income Taxes

Effective January 31, 1993, the Company adopted Statement of Financial Accounting Standards (SFAS) 109, "Accounting for Income Taxes." SFAS 109 requires a change from the deferred method of accounting for income taxes to the liability method. Under this method, deferred tax assets and liabilities are recognized based on the difference between the financial statement carrying amounts of existing assets and liabilities and their respective tax bases. Deferred tax assets and liabilities are measured using enacted tax rates in effect in the years in which those temporary differences are expected to reverse. Under SFAS 109, the effect on deferred taxes of a change in tax rates is recognized in income in the period that includes the enactment date. Under the deferred method, which was applied in 1992 and prior years, deferred income taxes are recognized for income and expense items that are reported in different years for financial reporting purposes and income tax purposes using the tax rate applicable for the year of calculation. Under the deferred method, deferred taxes are not adjusted for subsequent changes in tax rates.

Shareholders' Equity

Five hundred million shares of $.50 par value common stock are authorized, of which 357.8 million and 362.6 million were outstanding, net of 21.7 million shares and 16.8 million

FINANCIAL STRENGTH AND STABILITY GIVE US FREEDOM TO

shares held in treasury at January 29, 1994 and January 30, 1993. Ten million shares of $1.00 par value preferred stock are authorized, none of which has been issued.

Net Income Per Share

Net income per share is computed based upon the weighted average number of outstanding common shares, including the effect of stock options. There were 363.2 million, 363.7 million and 363.6 million weighted average outstanding shares for 1993, 1992 and 1991.

Issuance of Subsidiary Stock

Gains or losses resulting from stock issued by a subsidiary of the Company are recognized in current year's income. In 1992, the Company recognized a $9 million pre-tax gain which resulted from the March, 1992 initial public offering of the United Retail Group, Inc. A more detailed discussion of this matter is included under the heading "Gain on Issuance of United Retail Group, Inc. Stock" in Management's Discussion and Analysis on page 68 of this Annual Report.

2 Special and Nonrecurring Items

During 1993, the Company approved a restructuring plan which includes the following components: the sale of a 60% interest in the Brylane mail order business; the acceleration of store remodeling, downsizing and closing program at the Limited Stores and Lerner divisions; and the refocusing of the merchandise strategy at the Henri Bendel division.

On August 31, 1993, the Company sold 60% of its interest in the Brylane mail order business, receiving $285 million in cash proceeds. The transaction resulted in a pre-tax gain of approximately $203 million. Brylane distributes apparel through Lane Bryant Direct, Roaman's and Lerner Direct Catalogs.

To improve the underperforming divisions and expedite their turnaround, the Company decided to remodel and downsize a number of Limited and Lerner stores. The store remodels include both the expansion of store size and relocation of stores to other locations within the same mall. In either case, a remodel involves the destruction of certain existing assets. The downsizing of stores reduces the size of stores with substandard productivity and profit performance. The provision for remodels and downsizing aggregates approximately $35 million and includes the net book value of fixed asset writeoffs and lease termination payments.

In addition, the Company decided to close underperforming stores, primarily in the Lerner and Limited Stores retail businesses. These closings have been identified based on the profit performance of the store and an assessment of the quality of the real estate. The provision for store closings aggregates approximately $22 million and includes the operating losses through the date of closing, the net book value of abandoned fixed assets and lease termination payments.

This program includes the remodeling, downsizing and closing of approximately 360 Limited and Lerner stores by the end of 1995. The Company has closed approximately 60 of these stores and remodeled approximately 50 stores as of year-end.

The Company also estimated that, based on expected future cash flows, there was no expectation of realizing through future operations the existing carrying value of certain fixed and intangible assets at Lerner, Limited Stores and Henri Bendel, and other assets, and accordingly recorded a charge of approximately $143 million to reduce their net book value to an amount considered realizable in future periods.

The charges for these actions totalled approximately $200 million, of which approximately $173 million relates to non-cash charges for asset impairments, remodels and store closings.

A further discussion of this matter is included under the heading "Special and Non-recurring Items" in Management's Discussion and Analysis on page 67 of this Annual Report.

3 Accounts Receivable

Accounts receivable consisted of:

	1993	1992
Deferred payment accounts	$1,013,276	$755,822
Trade and other	78,532	106,528
Allowance for uncollectible accounts	(34,897)	(24,973)
	$1,056,911	$837,377

IMPLEMENT WHAT WE'VE LEARNED IN RESPONSE TO OUR CUST

Finance charge revenue on the deferred payment accounts amounted to $174.5 million, $141.8 million and $131.5 million in 1993, 1992 and 1991, and the provision for uncollectible accounts amounted to $50.8 million, $40.0 million and $50.6 million in 1993, 1992 and 1991. These amounts are classified as components of the cost to administer the deferred payment program and are included in general, administrative and store operating expenses.

4 Property and Equipment

Property and equipment, at cost, consisted of:

	1993	1992
Land, buildings and improvements	$510,998	$512,283
Furniture, fixtures and equipment	1,571,568	1,476,081
Leaseholds and improvements	506,258	677,115
Construction in progress	49,373	55,491
	2,638,197	2,720,970
Less: Accumulated depreciation and amortization	971,609	907,022
Property and equipment, net	$1,666,588	$1,813,948

5 Leased Facilities and Commitments

Annual store rent is comprised of a fixed minimum amount, plus contingent rent based upon a percentage of sales exceeding a stipulated amount. Store lease terms generally require additional payments covering taxes, common area costs and certain other expenses.

A summary of rent expense for 1993, 1992 and 1991 follows:

Store Rent:	1993	1992	1991
Fixed minimum	$540,381	$498,607	$380,291
Contingent	19,727	19,043	22,555
Total store rent	560,108	517,650	402,846
Equipment and other	31,897	37,228	38,734
Total rent expense	$592,005	$554,878	$441,580

At January 29, 1994, the Company was committed to noncancelable leases with remaining terms of one to forty years. A substantial portion of these commitments are store leases with initial terms ranging from ten to twenty years. Accrued rent expense was $99.1 million and $67.7 million at January 29, 1994 and January 30, 1993.

A summary of minimum rent commitments under noncancelable leases follows:

1994	$568,338
1995	559,356
1996	542,072
1997	523,249
1998	503,816
Thereafter	$2,695,394

6 Long-Term Debt

Long-term debt consisted of:

	1993	1992
Commercial Paper	$ –	$29,439
Certificates of Deposit	–	12,200
7½% Debentures due March, 2023	250,000	–
7.80% Notes due May, 2002	150,000	150,000
9¼% Notes due February, 2001	150,000	150,000
8⅞% Notes due August, 1999	100,000	100,000
8.61% Notes due December, 1993	–	100,000
	$650,000	$541,639

OMERS.

The Company maintains two revolving credit agreements (the "Agreements") totalling $840 million. One Agreement provides the Company available borrowings of up to $560 million. The other Agreement provides World Financial Network National Bank, a wholly-owned consolidated subsidiary, available borrowings of up to $280 million. Borrowings outstanding under the Agreements are due December 4, 1997. However, the revolving terms of each of the Agreements may be extended an additional two years upon notification by the Company on the second and fourth anniversaries of the Effective Date, subject to the approval of the lending banks. Both Agreements have similar borrowing options, including interest rates which are based on either the lenders' "Base Rate," as defined, LIBOR, CD-based options or at a rate submitted under a bidding process. Aggregate commitment and facility fees for the Agreements approximate 0.15% of the total commitment. Both Agreements and certain of the Company's other debt agreements place restrictions on the amount of the Company's working capital, debt and net worth. No amounts were outstanding under the Agreements at January 29, 1994.

Both Agreements support the Company's commercial paper program which funds working capital and other general corporate requirements. No commercial paper was outstanding at January 29, 1994.

In February, 1993, the Company amended its shelf registration statement enabling it to issue up to $500 million of debt securities and warrants to purchase debt securities. Following the $250 million issuance of 7½% Debentures due 2023 on March 15, 1993, the Company has $250 million remaining under its shelf registration statement authorization.

At January 30, 1993, the 8.61% Notes, the commercial paper and the certificates of deposit were classified as long-term based on the Company's intention and ability to refinance the obligations on a long-term basis. Following the $250 million issuance of 7½% Debentures in March, 1993, the Company retired the 8.61% Notes upon their maturity in December, 1993 and now classifies commercial paper and certificates of deposit as current liabilities based on their maturity.

All long-term debt outstanding at January 29, 1994 and January 30, 1993 is unsecured.

The Company periodically enters into interest rate swap agreements with the intent to manage the interest rate exposure of its debt portfolio. At January 29, 1994, the Company had two interest rate swap positions outstanding, each having a $100 million notional principal amount. One contract effectively changed the Company's interest rate exposure on $100 million of variable rate debt to a fixed rate of 8.09% through July, 2000. The counterparty to the swap contract has an option to cancel the remaining term of the contract in July, 1995. The second contract effectively changes the interest rate on $100 million of fixed rate debt to a variable rate through November, 1995.

No long-term debt matures in years 1994–1998. Interest paid approximated $57.4 million, $60.0 million and $58.2 million in 1993, 1992 and 1991.

7 Income Taxes

As discussed in Note 1, the Company adopted SFAS 109 effective January 31, 1993. No cumulative effect adjustment was required for the adoption as the difference in deferred income taxes under SFAS 109 and APB Opinion 11 was immaterial. The impact of adoption on the current year was also immaterial.

The provision for income taxes consisted of:

Currently Payable:	1993	1992	1991
Federal	$249,400	$174,900	$173,700
State	35,100	28,700	27,000
Foreign	6,400	6,400	4,500
	290,900	210,000	205,200
Deferred:			
Federal	(41,800)	62,700	41,800
State	4,900	17,300	10,000
	(36,900)	80,000	51,800
Total Provision	$254,000	$290,000	$257,000

OUR FINANCIAL GOALS REQUIRE US TO STRETCH BEYOND OUR

The foreign component of pre-tax income, arising principally from overseas sourcing operations, was $54.8 million, $58.7 million and $44.5 million in 1993, 1992 and 1991.

A reconciliation between the statutory Federal income tax rate and the effective income tax rate follows:

	1993	1992	1991
Federal income tax rate	**35.0%**	34.0%	34.0%
State income tax, net of Federal income tax effect	**4.0**	4.0	3.7
Other items, net	**.4**	.9	1.2
	39.4%	38.9%	38.9%

Income taxes payable included current deferred tax assets of $41.1 million and $19.6 million at January 29, 1994 and January 30, 1993. The effect of temporary differences which gives rise to deferred income tax balances at January 29, 1994 was as follows:

	Assets	Liabilities	Total
Excess of tax over book depreciation		$(123,539)	$(123,539)
Undistributed earnings of foreign affiliate		(103,485)	(103,485)
Investment in affiliate		(39,171)	(39,171)
State income taxes	$8,681		8,681
Bad debt reserve	11,022		11,022
Restructuring	25,092		25,092
Other	23,163	(35,735)	(12,572)
	$67,958	$(301,930)	$(233,972)

For the years 1992 and 1991, deferred income tax expense resulted from timing differences in the recognition of income and expense. The components of the deferred tax provision follow:

	1992	1991
Excess of tax over book depreciation	$45,400	$17,200
Other items, net	34,600	34,600
	$80,000	$51,800

Income tax payments approximated $291.3 million, $199.8 million and $212.4 million for 1993, 1992 and 1991.

8 Stock Options and Restricted Stock

Stock options are granted to officers and key associates based upon fair market value at the date of grant. Option activity for 1991, 1992 and 1993 follows:

	Number of Shares	Weighted Average Option Price Per Share
Outstanding Options, February 2, 1991	5,796,000	$14.26
Activity during 1991: Granted Exercised Cancelled	707,000 (1,187,000) (194,000)	$26.56 10.12 18.05
Outstanding Options, February 1, 1992	5,122,000	$16.49
Activity during 1992: Granted Exercised Cancelled	1,476,000 (772,000) (312,000)	$23.91 12.73 22.99
Outstanding Options, January 30, 1993	5,514,000	$18.57
Activity during 1993: Granted Exercised Cancelled	2,457,000 (431,000) (357,000)	$21.74 12.22 22.32
Outstanding Options, January 29, 1994	7,183,000	$19.87

The Company had approximately 5.3 million shares available for grant at January 29, 1994 as compared to 7.4 million shares available at January 30, 1993 and 8.5 million shares available at February 1, 1992. Approximately 7.2 million shares of the Company's common stock were reserved for outstanding options, of which 3.3 million were exercisable as of January 29, 1994.

NDIVIDUAL "COMFORT ZONES."

In 1993, 590,000 restricted shares of the Company's common stock were granted to certain officers and key associates. The market value of the shares at the date of grant amounted to $12.7 million and is recorded within treasury stock in the accompanying consolidated financial statements. The market value is being amortized as compensation expense over the vesting period which ranges from four to ten years. Compensation expense of $1.3 million was recorded in 1993.

9 Retirement Benefits

The Company sponsors a defined contribution retirement plan. Participation in this plan is available to all associates who have completed 1,000 or more hours of service with the Company during certain 12 month periods and attained the age of 21. Company contributions to this plan are based on a percentage of the associates' annual compensation. The cost of this plan was $25.9 million in 1993, $20.1 million in 1992 and $16.3 million in 1991.

10 Finance Subsidiary

World Financial Network National Bank, a wholly-owned consolidated finance subsidiary, provides private label credit card lines to the customers of certain retail affiliates. Condensed financial information of the finance subsidiary follows:

Assets	Jan. 29, 1994	Jan. 30, 1993
Credit card receivables, net of allowance for uncollectible accounts	$978,500	$731,000
Other assets, net	40,300	20,500
	$1,018,800	$751,500
Liabilities and Investment		
Certificates of deposit	$15,700	$12,200
Payable to wholly-owned subsidiaries and affiliates of The Limited, Inc.	18,200	6,400
Investment of The Limited, Inc.:		
Subordinated debt	902,700	665,200
Equity investment	82,200	67,700
	$1,018,800	$751,500

Holders of credit cards issued by the finance subsidiary are located throughout the United States, and have various available lines of credit which are subject to change by the finance subsidiary. The credit cards are used to purchase merchandise offered for sale by affiliates.

11 Disclosures About Fair Value of Financial Instruments

The following methods and assumptions were used to estimate the fair value of each class of financial instruments for which it is practicable to estimate that value:

Current assets and current liabilities

The fair value of cash and equivalents, short-term borrowings, accounts payable and accrued expenses approximate fair value because of their short maturity. The carrying amount of the credit card receivables approximates fair value due to the short maturity and because the average interest rate approximates current market origination rates.

Long-term debt

The fair value of the Company's long-term debt is estimated based on the quoted market prices for the same or similar issues or on the current rates offered to the Company for debt of the same remaining maturities.

Interest rate swap agreements

The fair value of interest rate swaps (used for hedging purposes) is the estimated amount that the Company would receive or pay to terminate the swap agreements at the reporting date, taking into account current interest rates and the current credit-worthiness of the swap counterparties.

OUR DEBT-TO-EQUITY RATIO IS 27%, INDICATING THAT

The estimated fair values of the Company's financial instruments are as follows:

	1993		1992	
	Carrying Amount	Fair Value	Carrying Amount	Fair Value
Long-term debt	$(650,000)	$(712,078)	$(541,639)	$(584,472)
Net interest rate swaps	$(13)	$(13,289)	$374	$(5,334)

12 Quarterly Financial Data (Unaudited)

Summarized quarterly financial results for 1993 and 1992 follow:

1993 Quarter	First	Second	Third	Fourth
Net Sales	$1,518,561	$1,689,055	$1,616,667	$2,420,805
Gross Income	380,727	427,710	447,048	703,350
Net Income	44,225	68,232	82,215	196,327
Net Income Per Share	$0.12	$0.19	$0.23	$0.54
1992 Quarter				
Net Sales	$1,415,625	$1,489,393	$1,611,320	$2,427,958
Gross Income	357,938	410,932	440,421	781,449
Net Income	51,525	80,073	79,995	243,904
Net Income Per Share	$0.14	$0.22	$0.22	$0.67

Market Price and Dividend Information

	Market Price		Cash Dividend Per Share
Fiscal Year 1993	High	Low	
4th Quarter	$23¼	$16⅝	$.09
3rd Quarter	24	20	.09
2nd Quarter	24⅞	19¾	.09
1st Quarter	$30	$21¼	$.09
Fiscal Year 1992			
4th Quarter	$29⅜	$22⅞	$.07
3rd Quarter	25½	19¾	.07
2nd Quarter	24⅜	19¼	.07
1st Quarter	$32⅞	$22	$.07

The Company's common stock is traded on the New York Stock Exchange ("LTD") and the London Stock Exchange. On January 29, 1994, there were 68,025 shareholders of record. However, when including active associates who participate in the Company's stock purchase plan, associates who own shares through Company sponsored retirement plans and others holding shares in broker accounts under street name, the Company estimates the shareholder base at approximately 131,000.

OUR DEBT IS SMALL, RELATIVE TO OUR SHAREHOLDERS'

Report of Independent Accountants

To the Board of Directors
and Shareholders
of The Limited, Inc.

We have audited the accompanying consolidated balance sheets of The Limited, Inc.
and subsidiaries as of January 29, 1994 and January 30, 1993, and the related consolidated
statements of income, shareholders' equity, and cash flows for each of the three fiscal years
in the period ended January 29, 1994 (appearing on pages 72 through 83). These financial
statements are the responsibility of the Company's management. Our responsibility is to
express an opinion on these financial statements based on our audits.

We conducted our audits in accordance with generally accepted auditing standards.
Those standards require that we plan and perform the audit to obtain reasonable assurance
about whether the financial statements are free of material misstatement. An audit includes
examining, on a test basis, evidence supporting the amounts and disclosures in the financial
statements. An audit also includes assessing the accounting principles used and significant
estimates made by management, as well as evaluating the overall financial statement presentation. We believe that our audits provide a reasonable basis for our opinion.

In our opinion, the financial statements referred to above present fairly, in all material
respects, the consolidated financial position of The Limited, Inc. and subsidiaries as of
January 29, 1994 and January 30, 1993 and the consolidated results of their operations and
their cash flows for each of the three fiscal years in the period ended January 29, 1994 in
conformity with generally accepted accounting principles.

COOPERS & LYBRAND

Columbus, Ohio
February 14, 1994

EQUITY BASE.   THE BEST IS YET TO COME. –LHW

Maytag Corporation

Management's Discussion and Analysis of Financial Condition and Results of Operations

Comparison of 1993 with 1992

The Company operates in two business segments, home appliances and vending equipment. The operations of the home appliance segment represented 95.0 percent of net sales in 1993 and 1992.

Consolidated net sales decreased 1.8 percent in 1993 compared to 1992. Although sales volumes in the United States increased due to improved consumer confidence, the overall decline in sales resulted from a decrease in European sales, less favorable currency conversions of sales outside the United States, and the absence of sales from the microwave oven operation that was sold in June 1992. North American home appliance sales increased 3.1 percent in spite of the absence of sales from the microwave oven operation. European sales decreased 22.1 percent from 1992 due to less favorable currency conversions and lower sales volumes due to some market share declines. Sales in the Company's vending equipment segment declined 5.3 percent from 1992 due to slow economic activity in Europe, cutbacks by domestic bottlers and increased competition.

Gross profit as a percent of sales increased to 24.2 percent from 23.1 percent in 1992. The increase in margins resulted principally from improvements in the North American Appliance Group. The improvement in the North American Appliance Group was primarily due to production efficiencies, reductions of certain employee related costs and some selective price increases. In addition, 1992 results for the North American Appliance Group included plant start-up costs. Gross margins in Hoover Europe declined primarily due to operating inefficiencies associated with previously announced plans to close a factory in Dijon, France and higher pension costs. Vending equipment margins improved in 1993 due to reductions in material, distribution and warranty costs from 1992. In 1994, although consolidated pension and postretirement medical costs are expected to increase due to a reduction in the discount rate assumption and lower pension assets, this is expected to be offset by other cost reductions.

Selling, general and administrative (S,G&A) expenses decreased to 17.2 percent in 1993 from 17.4 percent in 1992. The decline was principally due to cost efficiencies resulting from the reorganization of the North American Appliance Group. Special charges consisted of a $50 million pretax charge in the first quarter of 1993 to cover anticipated additional costs associated with two "free flights" promotional programs in Europe and a $95 million pretax charge in the third quarter of 1992 for a reorganization of U.S. and European operations. Total pretax charges relating to the "free flights" promotion programs in 1993 were $60.4 million ($50 million in a special charge and $10.4 million in S,G&A) and in 1992 were $12.2 million. See page 38 of the notes to the financial statements for a discussion of this matter. Offsetting a portion of the 1993 European "free flights" expenses in S,G&A was a $5 million reversal of excess reorganization reserves in Europe.

Operating income for 1993 totaled $158.9 million compared to $78.6 million in 1992. Before special charges, operating income would have been $208.9 million or 7.0 percent of sales in 1993 compared to $173.6 million or 5.7 percent of sales in 1992.

The decrease in the effective tax rate for 1993 was primarily due to the 1992 tax rate reflecting the impact of non-recoverable losses outside the United States. The notes to the financial statements include a reconciliation between the statutory tax and the actual tax provided.

Excluding special charges in 1993 and 1992 and the cumulative effect of accounting changes in 1992, net income would have been $81.3 million or $.76 per share in 1993 compared to net income of $65.4 million or $.62 per share in 1992.

In November 1992, the Financial Accounting Standards Board issued Statement No. 112 (FAS112), "Employers' Accounting for Postemployment Benefits." The new rules require recognition of specified postemployment benefits provided to former or inactive employees, such as severance pay, workers' compensation, supplemental employment benefits, disability benefits and continuation of healthcare and life insurance coverages. The Company has estimated that the cumulative effect of adopting FAS112, which will be recorded in the first quarter of 1994, will not have a material impact on annual earnings for 1994. The ongoing expenses associated with the adoption of the new rules are not expected to be material.

Comparison of 1992 with 1991

The Company operates in two business segments, home appliances and vending equipment. The operations of the home appliance segment represented 95.0 percent of net sales in 1992 and 1991.

Effective January 1, 1992, the Company adopted Statement of Financial Accounting Standards No. 106 (FAS106) "Employers' Accounting for Postretirement Benefits Other than Pensions." FAS106 requires companies to recognize the cost of postretirement benefits over an employee's service period. The Company's previous practice had been to recognize these costs as claims were received. The one-time transitional cost for adopting FAS106 resulted in an aftertax charge of $222 million or $2.09 per share in the first quarter of 1992. FAS106 also resulted in an additional pretax charge of approximately $24 million in 1992. Implementation of FAS106 had no impact on cash flows and the Company continues to pay the cost of postretirement benefits as claims are received. Also effective January 1, 1992, the Company adopted Statement of Financial Accounting Standards No. 109 (FAS109) "Accounting for Income Taxes." The adoption of FAS109 required a one-time aftertax charge of $85 million or $.80 per share. However, there was no cash flow impact of adopting the pronouncement since deferred taxes changed by a like amount. The one-time cumulative impact of adopting both FAS106 and FAS109 totaled $307 million or $2.89 per share.

Consolidated net sales increased 2.4 percent in 1992 compared to 1991. The overall sales increase, although partially offset by lower prices, was due to market share gains in most product categories and increased volume as a result of improved consumer confidence in the United States. Sales of the Company's home appliances within North America increased 2.7 percent from 1991. While European sales were 1.3 percent higher in 1992 compared to 1991, the majority of the increase is due to favorable currency translation with volume remaining flat. The Company's vending sales increased 10.4 percent in 1992, primarily due to increased volume within the United States.

Gross profit as a percent of sales decreased to 23.1 percent from 24.1 percent in 1991. The deterioration in margins was principally caused by additional expenses arising from the use of FAS106 as well as expenses related to a plant startup, new product introductions and price reductions. Excluding FAS106 charges, gross profit as a percent of sales would have been 23.8 percent for 1992.

Selling, general and administrative expenses as a percent of sales and before reorganization remained relatively level at 17.4 percent in 1992 and 17.7 percent in 1991. The slight decrease was caused primarily by increased sales in 1992.

During the third quarter of 1992, the Company provided for the costs of reorganizing its North American and European operations. In North America, several manufacturing facilities are being realigned, effectively combining expertise in research, engineering and product development. In addition, sales forces were reorganized and streamlined. The Company was also implementing a centralized distribution and order system for its North American operations designed to enhance customer service and operational efficiency. The effort in Europe was aimed at downsizing production capacity and streamlining sales, marketing, administration and distribution activities. This special charge reduced income before income taxes by $95 million or $.70 per share after tax.

Operating income for 1992 amounted to $78.6 million compared to $191.5 million in 1991. Before the special reorganization charge, 1992 operating income would have been $173.6 million or 5.7 percent of sales, down $17.9 million or 9.4 percent from 1991. The net operating loss of the Company's European operations in 1992 increased $66.2 million from 1991 primarily due to a provision of $55 million for reorganization expenses relating to plant closings and other organizational changes and the continuing recession in the United Kingdom.

Management's Discussion and Analysis of Financial Condition and Results of Operations – continued

Comparison of 1992 with 1991 – continued

The increase in the effective tax rate was primarily due to the effect of non-recoverable losses outside of the United States. The notes to the financial statements contain a reconciliation between the statutory tax and the actual tax provided.

Excluding the cumulative effect of accounting changes and reorganization expenses, for comparative purposes, net income would have been $65.4 million or $.62 per share compared to net income of $79 million or $.75 per share in 1991.

Liquidity and Capital Resources

Cash provided by operations in 1993 totaled $71.3 million compared to $183.1 million in 1992. The overall decrease resulted from the funding of expenditures relating to the reorganization of the North American and European operations, the Hoover Europe free flights promotions and working capital needs in the North American Appliance Group. Offsetting this decrease was a $42 million withdrawal from an overfunded pension plan in Europe and lower funding of an employee benefit trust. Current assets were 1.6 times current liabilities at December 31, 1993 and 1.8 times at December 31, 1992.

Gross capital expenditures in 1993 were $99.3 million compared to $129.9 million in 1992. The expenditures in 1993 were mainly related to improvements in product design and manufacturing processes and increases in manufacturing capacity. Capital spending in 1992 was higher as it included major plant start-up projects. Planned capital expenditures for 1994 approximate $110 million and relate to ongoing production improvements and product enhancements. Depreciation expense increased to $102.5 million in 1993 from $94.0 million in 1992 resulting from major capital projects completed near the end of 1992.

Significant investing and financing transactions related to capital expenditures, debt retirement

and dividend payments were funded through operations and the issuance of $5.5 million in medium term notes and a $139.0 million increase in notes payable and commercial paper borrowings. The Company also reduced long term debt by $94.4 million during 1993.

The Company has two credit facilities which support the Company's commercial paper program. Subject to certain exceptions, the credit agreements require the Company to maintain certain quarterly levels of consolidated tangible net worth, leverage ratios and interest coverage ratios. The Company was in compliance with all covenants at December 31, 1993 and expects to be in compliance with all covenants. The covenants become more stringent commencing in the first quarter of 1994. Additional funds available at December 31, 1993 under all credit agreements, applying the terms of the most restrictive covenant above, totaled $243 million.

Dividend payments in both 1993 and 1992 amounted to $53 million or $.50 per share. Dividends amounted to nine percent of average shareowners' equity in 1993 and seven percent in 1992.

Any funding requirements for future capital expenditures and other cash requirements in excess of cash generated from operations will be supplemented with issuance of debt securities and bank borrowings.

Impact of Inflation

The Company uses the LIFO method of accounting for approximately 79 percent of its inventories. Under this method, the cost of sales reported in the financial statements approximates current costs. The charges to operations for depreciation represent the allocation of historical costs incurred over past years and are significantly less than if they were

based upon current costs of productive capacity being consumed. Assets acquired in prior years will, of course, be replaced at higher costs but this will take place over several years. New higher-cost assets will result in higher depreciation charges, but in many cases due to technological improvements, there will be operating cost savings as well.

Statements of Consolidated Income (Loss)
Thousands of Dollars Except Per Share Data

	Year ended December 31		
	1993	1992	1991
Net sales	$2,987,054	$3,041,223	$2,970,626
Cost of sales	2,262,942	2,339,406	2,254,221
Gross profit	724,112	701,817	716,405
Selling, general and administrative expenses	515,234	528,250	524,898
Special charges	50,000	95,000	
Operating income	158,878	78,567	191,507
Interest expense	(75,364)	(75,004)	(75,159)
Other—net	6,356	3,983	7,069
Income before income taxes and cumulative effect of accounting changes	89,870	7,546	123,417
Income taxes	38,600	15,900	44,400
Income (loss) before cumulative effect of accounting changes	51,270	(8,354)	79,017
Cumulative effect of accounting changes for postretirement benefits other than pensions and income taxes		(307,000)	
Net income (loss)	$ 51,270	$ (315,354)	$ 79,017
Income (loss) per average share of Common stock:			
Income (loss) before cumulative effect of accounting changes	$ .48	$ (.08)	$ .75
Cumulative effect of accounting changes		$ (2.89)	
Net income (loss) per Common share	$ .48	$ (2.97)	$ .75

See notes to consolidated financial statements.

Statements of Consolidated Financial Condition
Thousands of Dollars

	December 31	
Assets	1993	1992
Current assets		
Cash and cash equivalents	$ 31,730	$ 57,032
Accounts receivable, less allowance— (1993—$15,629; 1992—$16,380)	532,353	476,850
Inventories	429,154	401,083
Deferred income taxes	46,695	52,261
Other current assets	16,919	28,309
Total current assets	1,056,851	1,015,535
Noncurrent assets		
Deferred income taxes	68,559	71,442
Pension investments	168,103	215,433
Intangibles, less allowance for amortization— (1993—$46,936; 1992—$37,614)	319,657	328,980
Other noncurrent assets	35,266	35,989
Total noncurrent assets	591,585	651,844
Property, plant and equipment		
Land	46,149	47,370
Buildings and improvements	288,590	286,368
Machinery and equipment	1,068,199	962,006
Construction in progress	44,753	90,847
	1,447,691	1,386,591
Less allowance for depreciation	626,629	552,480
Total property, plant and equipment	821,062	834,111
Total assets	$2,469,498	$2,501,490

Liabilities and Shareowners' Equity	December 31 1993	December 31 1992
Current liabilities		
Notes payable	$ 157,571	$ 19,886
Accounts payable	195,981	218,142
Compensation to employees	84,405	89,245
Accrued liabilities	178,015	180,894
Income taxes payable	16,193	11,323
Current maturities of long-term debt	18,505	43,419
Total current liabilities	650,670	562,909
Noncurrent liabilities		
Deferred income taxes	44,882	89,011
Long-term debt	724,695	789,232
Postretirement benefits other than pensions	391,635	380,376
Other noncurrent liabilities	70,835	80,737
Total noncurrent liabilities	1,232,047	1,339,356
Shareowners' equity		
Common stock:		
Authorized—200,000,000 shares (par value $1.25)		
Issued—117,150,593 shares, including shares in treasury	146,438	146,438
Additional paid-in capital	480,067	478,463
Retained earnings	325,823	328,122
Cost of Common stock in treasury (1993—10,430,833 shares;		
1992—10,545,915 shares)	(232,510)	(234,993)
Employee stock plans	(62,342)	(65,638)
Foreign currency translation	(70,695)	(53,167)
Total shareowners' equity	586,781	599,225
Total liabilities and shareowners' equity	$2,469,498	$2,501,490

See notes to consolidated financial statements.

Statements of Consolidated Cash Flows
Thousands of Dollars

| | Year ended December 31 | | |
	1993	1992	1991
Operating activities			
Net income (loss)	$ 51,270	$(315,354)	$ 79,017
Adjustments to reconcile net income (loss) to net cash provided by operating activities:			
Cumulative effect of accounting changes		307,000	
Depreciation and amortization	111,781	103,351	92,667
Deferred income taxes	(35,833)	(30,210)	1,700
Reorganization expenses	(5,000)	95,000	
"Free flights" promotion expenses	60,379	12,235	
Changes in selected working capital items:			
Inventories	(29,323)	80,731	37,075
Receivables and other current assets	(48,609)	(6,051)	12,867
Reorganization reserve	(39,671)	(15,530)	
"Free flights" promotion reserve	(42,981)	(1,604)	
Other current liabilities	(17,383)	(70,422)	46,623
Net change in pension assets and liabilities	43,513	(12,149)	(22,385)
Postretirement benefits	11,259	21,254	
Other—net	11,913	14,814	(12,894)
Net cash provided by operations	71,315	183,065	234,670
Investing activities			
Capital expenditures—net	(95,990)	(120,364)	(138,100)
Total investing activities	(95,990)	(120,364)	(138,100)
Financing activities			
Proceeds from credit agreements and long-term borrowings	5,500	73,712	57,900
Increase (decrease) in notes payable	138,951	(2,378)	(31,023)
Reduction in long-term debt	(94,449)	(70,158)	(92,832)
Stock options exercised and other Common stock transactions	5,903	5,558	3,421
Dividends	(53,569)	(53,269)	(53,150)
Total financing activities	2,336	(46,535)	(115,684)
Effect of exchange rates on cash	(2,963)	(7,886)	(1,721)
Increase (decrease) in cash and cash equivalents	(25,302)	8,280	(20,835)
Cash and cash equivalents at beginning of year	57,032	48,752	69,587
Cash and cash equivalents at end of year	$ 31,730	$ 57,032	$ 48,752

See notes to consolidated financial statements.

Notes to Consolidated Financial Statements

Summary of Significant Accounting Policies:

Principles of Consolidation: The consolidated financial statements include the accounts and transactions of the Company and its wholly owned subsidiaries. Certain subsidiaries located outside the United States are consolidated as of a date one month earlier than subsidiaries in the United States. Intercompany accounts and transactions are eliminated in consolidation.

Exchange rate fluctuations from translating the financial statements of subsidiaries located outside the United States into U.S. dollars and exchange gains and losses from designated foreign currency transactions are recorded in a separate component of shareowners' equity. All other foreign exchange gains and losses are included in income.

Certain reclassifications have been made to prior years' financial statements to conform with the 1993 presentation.

Cash Equivalents: Highly liquid investments with a maturity of 90 days or less when purchased are considered by the Company to be cash equivalents.

Inventories: Inventories are stated at the lower of cost or market. Cost is determined by the last-in, first-out (LIFO) method for approximately 79% and 76% of the Company's inventories at December 31, 1993 and 1992. The remaining inventories, which are primarily outside the United States, are stated using the first-in, first-out (FIFO) method.

Intangibles: Intangibles principally represent goodwill, which is the cost of business acquisitions in excess of the fair value of identifiable net tangible assets. Goodwill is amortized over 40 years on the straight-line basis and the carrying value is reviewed annually. If this review indicates that goodwill will not be recoverable as determined based on the undiscounted cash flows of the entity acquired over the remaining amortization period, the Company's carrying value of the goodwill will be reduced by the estimated shortfall of cash flows.

Income Taxes: Certain expenses (principally related to accelerated tax depreciation, employee benefits and various other accruals) are recognized in different periods for financial reporting and income tax purposes.

Property, Plant and Equipment: Property, plant and equipment is stated on the basis of cost. Depreciation expense is calculated principally on the straight-line method for financial reporting purposes. The depreciation methods are designed to amortize the cost of the assets over their estimated useful lives.

Short and Long-Term Debt: The carrying amounts of the Company's borrowings under its short-term revolving credit agreements, including multicurrency loans, approximate their fair value. The fair values of the Company's long-term debt are estimated based on quoted market prices of comparable instruments.

Inventories

In thousands	1993	1992
Finished products	$282,841	$249,289
Work in process, raw materials and supplies	146,313	151,794
	$429,154	$401,083

If the first-in, first-out (FIFO) method of inventory accounting, which approximates current cost, had been used for all inventories, they would have been $76.3 million and $78.1 million higher than reported at December 31, 1993 and 1992.

Notes to Consolidated Financial Statements – continued

Pension Benefits

The Company and its subsidiaries have noncontributory defined benefit pension plans covering most employees. Plans covering salaried and management employees generally provide pension benefits that are based on an average of the employee's earnings and credited service. Plans covering hourly employees generally provide benefits of stated amounts for each year of service. The Company's funding policy is to contribute amounts to the plans sufficient to meet minimum funding requirements.

A summary of the components of net periodic pension expense (income) for the defined benefit plans is as follows:

	Year ended December 31		
In thousands	1993	1992	1991
Service cost—benefits earned during the period	$ 24,067	$ 21,469	$ 23,520
Interest cost on projected benefit obligation	90,322	87,654	85,325
Actual return on plan assets	(167,539)	(87,263)	(141,918)
Net amortization and deferral	59,315	(25,239)	23,602
Net pension expense (income)	$ 6,165	$ (3,379)	$ (9,471)

The change in pension expense (income) from 1992 to 1993 resulted from pension benefit improvements, a reduction in the discount rate and lower expected return on assets resulting from lower asset values at the beginning of the year.

Assumptions used in determining net periodic pension expense (income) for the defined benefit plans in the United States were:

	1993	1992	1991
Discount rates	8.5%	9%	9%
Rates of compensation increase	6	6	6
Expected long-term rates of return on assets	9.5	9.5	9.5

For the valuation of pension obligations at the end of 1993 and for determining pension expense in 1994, the discount rate and rate of compensation increase have been decreased to 7.5% and 5.0% respectively. Assumptions for defined benefit plans outside the United States are comparable to the above in all periods.

As of December 31, 1993, approximately 87% of the plan assets are invested in listed stocks and bonds. The balance is invested in real estate and short term investments.

Certain pension plans in the United States provide that in the event of a change of Company control and plan termination, any excess funding may be used only to provide pension benefits or to fund retirees' health care benefits. The use of all pension assets for anything other than providing employee benefits is either limited by legal restrictions or subject to severe taxation.

Pension Benefits – continued

The following table sets forth the funded status and amounts recognized in the statements of consolidated financial condition for the Company's defined benefit pension plans:

In thousands	December 31, 1993		December 31, 1992	
	Plans in Which Assets Exceed Accumulated Benefits	Plans in Which Accumulated Benefits Exceed Assets	Plans in Which Assets Exceed Accumulated Benefits	Plans in Which Accumulated Benefits Exceed Assets
Actuarial present value of benefit obligation:				
Vested benefit obligation	$(1,004,740)	$(15,474)	$ (889,570)	$(28,990)
Accumulated benefit obligation	$(1,084,352)	$(16,380)	$ (942,303)	$(29,009)
Projected benefit obligation	$(1,163,073)	$(18,989)	$(1,015,813)	$(31,186)
Plan assets at fair value	1,213,315	569	1,156,506	12,897
Projected benefit obligation less than (in excess of) plan assets	50,242	(18,420)	140,693	(18,289)
Unrecognized net loss	41,037	1,046	47,244	1,087
Prior service cost not yet recognized in net periodic pension cost	110,024	3,272	66,571	2,066
Unrecognized net obligation (asset) at adoption of FASB 87, net of amortization	(38,128)	1,647	(43,602)	1,729
Net pension investment (liability)	163,175	(12,455)	210,906	(13,407)
Minimum liability adjustment	4,928	(4,928)	4,527	(4,527)
Pension investment (liability) recognized in the statements of consolidated financial condition	$ 168,103	$(17,383)	$ 215,433	$(17,934)

Pension investments above of approximately $104 million and $142 million at December 31, 1993 and 1992, and pension income of $5.4 million, $10.9 million and $7.1 million in 1993, 1992 and 1991 relate to pension plans covering employees in Europe.

In 1993 and 1992, the Company recorded $4.9 million and $4.5 million, respectively, to recognize the minimum pension liability required by the provisions of Statement of Financial Accounting Standards No. 87, "Employers' Accounting for Pensions." The transaction, which had no effect on income, was offset by recording an intangible asset of an equivalent amount.

Notes to Consolidated Financial Statements – continued

Postretirement Benefits Other Than Pensions

In addition to providing pension benefits, the Company provides postretirement health care and life insurance benefits for its employees in the United States. Most of the postretirement plans are contributory, and contain certain other cost sharing features such as deductibles and coinsurance. The plans are unfunded. Employees are not vested and these benefits are subject to change. Death benefits for certain retired employees are funded as part of, and paid out of, pension plans.

In 1992, the Company adopted Statement of Financial Accounting Standards No. 106, "Employers' Accounting for Postretirement Benefits Other Than Pensions," which requires employers to accrue the cost of such retirement benefits during the employee's service with the Company. Prior to 1992, the cost of providing these benefits to retired employees was recognized as a charge to income as claims were received. The transition obligation of $355 million as of January 1, 1992 was recorded as a one-time charge in the first quarter of 1992 and reduced net income by $222 million or $2.09 per share. The ongoing effect of adopting the new standard increased 1993 and 1992 periodic postretirement benefit cost by $11.3 and $23.9 million respectively. Postretirement benefit costs in 1991 of approximately $11.7 million were recorded on a cash basis and have not been restated.

A summary of the components of net periodic postretirement benefit cost is as follows:

In thousands	1993	1992
Service cost	$10,225	$ 8,258
Interest cost	26,939	30,421
Net amortization and deferral	(8,228)	2,106
Net periodic postretirement benefit cost	$28,936	$40,785

Postretirement benefit costs for 1993 decreased primarily due to a plan amendment to eligibility requirements.

Assumptions used in determining net periodic postretirement benefit cost were:

	1993	1992
Health care cost trend rates (1):		
Current year	14%	15%
Decreasing gradually to	6%	6%
Until the year	2009	2009
Each year thereafter	6%	6%
Discount rates	8.5%	9.0%

(1) Weighted-average annual assumed rate of increase in the per capita cost of covered benefits.

For the valuation of the accumulated benefit obligation at December 31, 1993 and for determining postretirement benefit costs in 1994, the health care cost trend rates were decreased. This results in a health care cost trend rate of 12.5 percent in 1994, decreasing gradually to 6 percent until 2001 and remaining at that level thereafter. In addition, the discount rate was reduced to 7.5 percent.

The health care cost trend rate assumption has a significant impact on the amounts reported. For example, increasing the assumed health care cost trend rates by one percentage point in each year would increase the accumulated postretirement benefit obligation as of December 31, 1993 by $43.6 million and the aggregate of the service and interest cost components of net periodic postretirement benefit cost for 1993 by $5.9 million.

Postretirement Benefits Other Than Pensions – continued

The following table presents the status of the plans reconciled with amounts recognized in the statements of consolidated financial condition for the Company's postretirement benefits.

	December 31	
In thousands	1993	1992
Accumulated postretirement benefit obligation:		
Retirees	$284,524	$189,764
Fully eligible active plan participants	58,709	60,236
Other active plan participants	56,465	76,587
	399,698	326,587
Unamortized plan amendment	54,248	62,476
Unrecognized net loss	(62,311)	(8,687)
Postretirement benefit liability recognized in the statements of consolidated financial condition	$391,635	$380,376

Other Employee Benefits

The Company has a leveraged employee stock ownership plan (ESOP) for eligible United States employees. The ESOP is designed to fund the Company's contribution to an existing salaried savings plan. The Company made contributions to the plan of $5.5 million, $5.2 million and $4.9 million for loan payments in 1993, 1992 and 1991, the majority of which represents interest on the ESOP debt. With each loan and interest payment, a portion of the Common stock in the ESOP becomes available for allocation to participating employees.

The Company also sponsors other defined contribution plans. Contributions to these plans are generally based on employees' compensation. Expenses of the Company related to these plans, including the ESOP, amounted to $8.6 million in 1993, $7.9 million in 1992 and $7.8 million in 1991.

In November 1992, the Financial Accounting Standards Board issued Statement No. 112 (FAS112), "Employers' Accounting for Postemployment Benefits." The new rules require recognition of specified postemployment benefits provided to former or inactive employees, such as severance pay, workers' compensation, supplemental employment benefits, disability benefits and continuation of health care and life insurance coverages. The Company has estimated the cumulative effect of adopting FAS112, which will be recorded in the first quarter of 1994, will not have a material impact on the annual results for 1994. The ongoing expenses associated with the new statement are not expected to be material.

Accrued Liabilities

In thousands	1993	1992
Warranties	$ 46,281	$ 50,877
Advertising/sales promotion	51,946	30,054
Other	79,788	99,963
	$178,015	$180,894

Notes to Consolidated Financial Statements – continued

Income Taxes

Effective January 1, 1992, the Company adopted Statement of Financial Accounting Standards No. 109, "Accounting for Income Taxes," which requires recognition of deferred tax liabilities and assets for the expected future tax consequences of events that have been included in the financial statements or tax returns. Under this method, deferred tax liabilities and assets are determined based on the difference between the financial statement and tax bases of assets and liabilities using enacted tax rates in effect for the year in which the differences are expected to reverse. Prior to 1992, the provision for income taxes was based on income

and expenses included in the accompanying consolidated statements of income. As permitted under the new rules, prior years' financial statements have not been restated. The cumulative effect of adopting Statement 109 was to decrease net income by $85 million or $.80 per share as of January 1, 1992.

At December 31, 1993, the Company has available for tax purposes approximately $177 million of net operating loss carryforwards outside the United States, of which $38 million expire in various years through 1999 and $139 million is available indefinitely. Of this amount, $30 million relates to pre-acquisition net operating losses which will be used to reduce intangibles when utilized.

Deferred income taxes reflect the net tax effects of temporary differences between the amount of assets and liabilities for financial reporting purposes and the amounts used for income tax purposes. Significant components of the Company's deferred tax assets and liabilities as of December 31, 1993 and 1992 are as follows:

In thousands	1993	1992
Deferred tax assets (liabilities):		
Tax over book depreciation	$(118,973)	$(116,725)
Postretirement benefit obligation	151,424	143,197
Product warranty accruals	20,021	20,221
Pensions and other employee benefits	(38,753)	(58,704)
Reorganization accrual	8,856	23,586
Net operating loss carryforwards	48,817	23,178
Other	14,937	15,812
	86,329	50,565
Less valuation allowance for deferred tax assets	(15,957)	(15,873)
Net deferred tax assets	$ 70,372	$ 34,692
Recognized in statements of consolidated financial condition:		
Deferred tax assets—current	$ 46,695	$ 52,261
Deferred tax assets—noncurrent	68,559	71,442
Deferred tax liabilities	(44,882)	(89,011)
Net deferred tax assets	$ 70,372	$ 34,692

Income (loss) before income taxes and cumulative effect of accounting changes consists of the following:

	Year ended December 31		
In thousands	1993	1992	1991
United States	$162,554	$ 80,013	$112,988
Non-United States	(72,684)	(72,467)	10,429
	$ 89,870	$ 7,546	$123,417

Income Taxes – continued

Significant components of the provision for income taxes are as follows:

In thousands	Year ended December 31		
	1993	1992	1991
Current provision:			
Federal	$ 51,700	$ 37,000	$28,600
State	9,100	7,100	6,000
Non-United States	20,000	2,000	8,100
	80,800	46,100	42,700
Deferred provision:			
Federal	400	(13,800)	7,600
State	700	(3,100)	
Non-United States	(43,300)	(13,300)	(5,900)
	(42,200)	(30,200)	1,700
Provision for income taxes	$ 38,600	$ 15,900	$44,400

Significant items impacting the effective income tax rate follow:

In thousands	Year ended December 31		
	1993	1992	1991
Income before cumulative effect of accounting changes computed at the statutory United States income tax rate	$31,500	$ 2,600	$42,000
Increase (reduction) resulting from:			
Acquisitions:			
Intangibles amortization	3,200	3,100	3,100
Depreciation			2,400
The effect of statutory rate differences outside the United States	2,500	2,600	600
Non-United States losses with no tax benefit		10,700	
State income taxes, net of federal tax benefit	6,400	2,700	4,000
Tax credits arising outside the United States	(800)	(5,400)	(7,300)
Effect of tax rate changes on deferred taxes	(2,500)		
Other—net	(1,700)	(400)	(400)
Provision for income taxes	$38,600	$15,900	$44,400

Since the Company plans to continue to finance expansion and operating requirements of subsidiaries outside the United States through reinvestment of the undistributed earnings of these subsidiaries (approximately $81 million at December 31, 1993), taxes which would result from distribution have not been provided on such earnings. If such earnings were distributed, additional taxes payable would be significantly reduced by available tax credits arising from taxes paid outside the United States.

Income taxes paid, net of refunds received, during 1993, 1992 and 1991 were $68.3 million, $28.5 million and $34.5 million, respectively.

Notes to Consolidated Financial Statements – continued

Long-Term Debt and Notes Payable

The following sets forth the long-term debt in the statements of consolidated financial condition:

In thousands	1993	1992
Notes payable with interest payable semiannually:		
Due May 15, 2002 at 9.75%	$200,000	$200,000
Due July 15, 1999 at 8.875%	175,000	175,000
Due July 1, 1997 at 8.875%	100,000	100,000
Medium-term notes, maturing from 1994 to 2010, from		
7.69% to 9.03% with interest payable semiannually	177,750	197,250
Employee stock ownership plan notes payable semiannually		
through July 2, 2004 at 9.35%	59,129	60,307
Multicurrency loans at 5.4% to 9.475%		63,631
Other	31,321	36,463
	743,200	832,651
Less current portion	18,505	43,419
	$724,695	$789,232

The 9.75% notes, the 8.875% notes due in 1999 and the medium-term notes grant the holders the right to require the Company to repurchase all or any portion of their notes at 100% of the principal amount thereof, together with accrued interest, following the occurrence of both a change in Company control and a credit rating decline.

The Company has established a trust to administer a leveraged employee stock ownership plan (ESOP) within an existing employee savings plan. The Company has guaranteed the debt of the trust and will service the repayment of the notes, including interest, through the Company's employee savings plan contribution and from the quarterly dividends paid on stock held by the ESOP. Dividends paid by the Company on stock held by the ESOP totaled $1.4 million in 1993, 1992 and 1991. The ESOP notes are secured by the Common stock owned by the ESOP trust.

The fair value of the Company's long-term debt, based on public quotes if available, exceeded the amount recorded in the statements of consolidated financial condition at December 31, 1993 and 1992 by $83.7 million and $50 million, respectively.

Notes payable at December 31, 1993 and 1992 consisted of notes payable to banks, in addition to $112 million in commercial paper borrowings at December 31, 1993. The Company's commercial paper program is supported by two credit agreements totaling $300 million, which were entered into on June 25, 1993. The $100 million agreement expires June 24, 1994 and the $200 million agreement expires June 25, 1996. Subject to certain exceptions, the credit agreements require the Company to maintain certain quarterly levels of consolidated tangible net worth, leverage ratios and interest coverage ratios. At December 31, 1993, the Company was in compliance with all covenants. Additional funds available at December 31, 1993 under all credit agreements, applying the terms of the most restrictive covenant, totaled $243 million.

Interest paid during 1993, 1992 and 1991 was $76.2 million, $77.4 million, and $78.4 million. The aggregate maturities of long-term debt in each of the next five fiscal years is as follows (in thousands): 1994-$18,505; 1995-$45,185; 1996-$5,308; 1997-$106,535; 1998-$7,147.

Stock Plans

In 1992, the shareowners approved the 1992 stock option plan for executives and key employees. The plan provides that options could be granted to key employees for not more than 3.6 million shares of the Common stock of the Company. The option price under the plan is the fair market value at the date of the grant. Options may not be exercised until one year after the date granted.

Under the Company's 1986 plan which expired in 1991, options to purchase 1.6 million shares of Common stock were granted at the market value at the date of grant. Some options were also granted under this plan with stock appreciation rights (SAR) which entitle the employee to surrender the right to receive up to one-half of the shares covered by the option and to receive a cash payment equal to the difference between the option price and the market value of the shares being surrendered. Under a plan which expired in 1986, options to purchase 800,000 shares of Common stock were granted at the market value at date of grant.

In April 1990, the Company's shareowners approved the Maytag Corporation 1989 Stock Option Plan for Non-Employee Directors which authorizes the issuance of up to 250,000 shares of Common stock to the Company's non-employee directors. Options under this plan are immediately exercisable upon grant.

The following is a summary of certain information relating to these plans:

	Average Price	Option Shares	SAR
Outstanding December 31, 1990	$14.81	966,851	459,131
Granted	14.76	885,920	246,240
Exercised	10.49	(7,526)	
Canceled or expired	17.59	(18,450)	(12,988)
Outstanding December 31, 1991	14.76	1,826,795	692,383
Granted	14.54	411,910	
Exercised	9.86	(179,736)	(11,192)
Exchanged for SAR	11.16	(11,192)	
Canceled or expired	12.63	(34,640)	(93,242)
Outstanding December 31, 1992	15.09	2,013,137	587,949
Granted	15.92	599,060	
Exercised	12.89	(101,156)	(5,360)
Exchanged for SAR	12.53	(5,360)	
Canceled or expired	16.26	(147,080)	(85,728)
Outstanding December 31, 1993	$15.33	2,358,601	496,861

Options for 1,777,361 shares, 1,623,227 shares and 964,875 shares were exercisable at December 31, 1993, 1992 and 1991. There were 2,784,030 shares available for future grants at December 31, 1993. In the event of a change in Company control, all stock options granted become immediately exercisable.

In 1991, the shareowners approved the 1991 Stock Incentive Award Plan For Key Executives. This plan authorizes the issuance of up to 2.5 million shares of Common stock to certain key employees of the Company, of which 1,980,338 shares are available for future grants as of December 31, 1993. Under the terms of the plan, the granted stock vests three years after the award date and is contingent upon pre-established performance objectives. In the event of a change in Company control, all incentive stock awards become fully vested. No incentive stock awards may be granted under this plan on or after May 1, 1996. Incentive stock award shares outstanding at December 31, 1993 under a 1993 grant total 459,957, and $3.6 million has been expensed during 1993 for the anticipated payout on these awards. Under a 1991 grant which expired in 1993, 53,068 shares are vested and outstanding and $1.1 million has been expensed during 1993. No amounts were expensed in 1992 and 1991 under these awards.

Notes to Consolidated Financial Statements – continued

Shareowners' Equity

In thousands	Common Stock Shares	Common Stock Amount	Additional Paid-in Capital	Retained Earnings	Treasury Stock Shares	Treasury Stock Amount	Employee Stock Plans	Foreign Currency Translation
Balance 12/31/90	117,151	$146,438	$487,034	$670,878	(11,424)	$(254,576)	$(63,590)	$ 28,547
Net income				79,017				
Cash dividends				(53,150)				
Stock issued under employee stock plans			(50)		8	168		
Stock awards:								
Granted			(6,953)		588	13,110	(6,157)	
Earned or canceled			96		(17)	(376)	2,130	
Conversion of subordinated debentures			7		(1)	(22)		
ESOP:								
Issued			(301)		38	848		
Allocated							906	
Translation adjustments								(33,419)
Balance 12/31/91	117,151	146,438	479,833	696,745	(10,808)	(240,848)	(66,711)	(4,872)
Net loss				(315,354)				
Cash dividends				(53,269)				
Stock issued under employee stock plans			(1,221)		178	3,970		
Stock awards:								
Granted			(204)		41	921	(718)	
Earned or canceled			524		(44)	(970)	446	
ESOP:								
Issued			(469)		87	1,934		
Allocated							1,345	
Translation adjustments								(48,295)
Balance 12/31/92	117,151	146,438	478,463	328,122	(10,546)	(234,993)	(65,638)	(53,167)
Net income				51,270				
Cash dividends				(53,569)				
Stock issued under employee stock plans			(911)		92	2,111		
Stock awards:								
Granted			(3,645)		491	10,939	(7,294)	
Earned or canceled			6,136		(550)	(12,403)	9,102	
ESOP:								
Issued			(651)		82	1,836		
Allocated							1,488	
Tax benefit of ESOP dividends and stock options			675					
Translation adjustments								(17,528)
Balance 12/31/93	117,151	$146,438	$480,067	$325,823	(10,431)	$(232,510)	$(62,342)	$(70,695)

Shareowners' Equity – continued

The Company has 24 million authorized shares of Preferred stock, par value $1 per share, none of which is issued.

Pursuant to a Shareholder Rights Plan approved by the Company in 1988, each share of Common stock carries with it one Right. Until exercisable, the Rights will not be transferable apart from the Company's Common stock. When exercisable, each Right will entitle its holder to purchase one one-hundredth of a share of Preferred stock of the Company at a price of $75. The Rights will only become exercisable if a person or group acquires 20% or more of the Company's Common stock which may be reduced to not less than 10% at the discretion of the Board of Directors. In the event the Company is acquired in a merger or 50% or more of its consolidated assets or earnings power are sold, each Right entitles the holder to purchase Common stock of either the surviving or acquired company at one-half its market price. The Rights may be redeemed in whole by the Company at a purchase price of $.01 per Right. The Preferred shares will be entitled to 100 times the aggregate per share dividend payable on the Company's Common stock and to 100 votes on all matters submitted to a vote of shareowners. The Rights expire May 2, 1998.

Industry Segment and Geographic Information

Principal financial data by industry segment is as follows:

In thousands	1993	1992	1991
Net Sales			
Home appliances	$2,830,457	$2,875,902	$2,820,828
Vending equipment	156,597	165,321	149,798
Total	$2,987,054	$3,041,223	$2,970,626
Income (Loss) Before Income Taxes and Cumulative			
Effect of Accounting Changes			
Home appliances	$ 160,431	$ 62,568	$ 187,018
Vending equipment	17,566	16,311	4,498
Corporate (including interest expense)	(88,127)	(71,333)	(68,099)
Total	$ 89,870	$ 7,546	$ 123,417
Capital Expenditures—net			
Home appliances	$ 92,194	$ 115,676	$ 133,504
Vending equipment	1,028	771	4,612
Corporate	2,768	3,917	(16)
Total	$ 95,990	$ 120,364	$ 138,100
Depreciation and Amortization			
Home appliances	$ 105,916	$ 98,116	$ 86,928
Vending equipment	4,377	4,236	4,805
Corporate	1,488	999	934
Total	$ 111,781	$ 103,351	$ 92,667
Identifiable Assets			
Home appliances	$2,147,174	$2,135,961	$2,200,227
Vending equipment	103,765	104,119	119,752
Corporate	218,559	261,410	215,089
Total	$2,469,498	$2,501,490	$2,535,068

Notes to Consolidated Financial Statements – continued

Industry Segment and Geographic Information – continued

Information about the Company's operations in different geographic locations is as follows:

In thousands	1993	1992	1991
Net Sales			
North America	$2,468,374	$2,407,591	$2,332,365
Europe	390,761	501,857	495,517
Other	127,919	131,775	142,744
Total	$2,987,054	$3,041,223	$2,970,626
Income (Loss) Before Income Taxes and Cumulative			
Effect of Accounting Changes			
North America	$ 246,981	$ 145,991	$ 190,820
Europe	(72,358)	(67,061)	(865)
Other	3,374	(51)	1,561
Corporate (including interest expense)	(88,127)	(71,333)	(68,099)
Total	$ 89,870	$ 7,546	$ 123,417
Identifiable Assets			
North America	$1,794,271	$1,677,131	$1,681,304
Europe	359,323	452,995	507,746
Other	97,345	109,954	130,929
Corporate	218,559	261,410	215,089
Total	$2,469,498	$2,501,490	$2,535,068

Sales between affiliates of different geographic regions are not significant. The amount of exchange gain or loss included in operations in any of the years presented was not material.

In 1993 the Company incurred $60.4 million in pretax charges for two "free flights" promotion programs in Europe ($50 million in a special charge and $10.4 million in selling, general and adminis-trative expenses.) In 1992 the Company incurred $95 million of reorganization expenses for marketing and distribution changes in North America and plant closings and other organizational changes in Europe. Of the $95 million allocated to Home Appliances, $40 million was allocated to North America and $55 million to Europe.

Contingent Liabilities

In 1993 and 1992, the Company made provisions to cover the cost of two Hoover Europe "free flights" promotion programs, including a $50 million special charge in the first quarter of 1993. The promotions began in August, 1992 and included qualified purchases through January, 1993. The terms of the promotions require all flights to commence before the end of the second quarter of 1994. The Company believes that it has made adequate provisions for any costs to be incurred relating to these promotions. Although the final costs of the promotions cannot be determined at this time, management does not believe that any additional costs that may be incurred will have a material adverse effect on the financial condition of the Company.

At December 31, 1993, the Company is contingently liable for guarantees of indebtedness owed by a third party ("the borrower") of $21.3 million relating to the sale of one of its manufacturing facilities in 1992. The borrower is performing under the payment terms of the loan agreement; however, it was out of compliance with certain financial covenants at December 31, 1993 for which it has requested a waiver from the lender involved. The indebtedness is collateralized by the assets of the borrower.

Other contingent liabilities arising in the normal course of business, including guarantees, repurchase agreements, pending litigation, environmental issues, taxes and other claims are not considered to be material in relation to the Company's financial position.

Report of Independent Auditors

Shareowners and Board of Directors
Maytag Corporation

We have audited the accompanying statements of consolidated financial condition of Maytag Corporation and subsidiaries as of December 31, 1993 and 1992, and the related statements of consolidated income and consolidated cash flows for each of the three years in the period ended December 31, 1993. These financial statements are the responsibility of the Company's management. Our responsibility is to express an opinion on these financial statements based on our audits.

We conducted our audits in accordance with generally accepted auditing standards. Those standards require that we plan and perform the audit to obtain reasonable assurance about whether the financial statements are free of material misstatement. An audit includes examining, on a test basis, evidence supporting the amounts and disclosures in the financial statements. An audit also includes assessing the accounting principles used and significant estimates made by management, as well as evaluating the overall financial statement presentation. We believe that our audits provide a reasonable basis for our opinion.

In our opinion, the financial statements referred to above present fairly, in all material respects, the consolidated financial position of Maytag Corporation and subsidiaries at December 31, 1993 and 1992, and the results of their operations and their cash flows for each of the three years in the period ended December 31, 1993, in conformity with generally accepted accounting principles.

As discussed in notes to consolidated financial statements, in 1992 the Company changed its method of accounting for postretirement benefits other than pensions and income taxes.

Ernst + Young

Chicago, Illinois
February 1, 1994

Quarterly Results of Operations (Unaudited)

The following is a summary of unaudited quarterly results of operations for the years ended December 31, 1993 and 1992.

In thousands except per share data	December 31	September 30	June 30	March 31
1993				
Net sales	$746,723	$770,222	$753,256	$716,853
Gross profit	179,066	188,501	183,812	172,733
Net income (loss)	17,469	23,040	21,307	(10,546)
Per average share	$ .16	$ .22	$ .20	$ (.10)
1992				
Net sales	$782,446	$735,540	$770,060	$753,177
Gross profit	173,495	161,871	176,803	189,648
Income (loss) before cumulative effect of accounting changes	11,238	(63,234)	18,937	24,705
Per average share	.11	(.60)	.18	.23
Net income (loss)	11,238	(63,234)	18,937	(282,295)
Per average share	$ .11	$ (.60)	$ .18	$ (2.66)

The quarter ended March 31, 1993 includes a $50 million pretax special charge for additional costs associated with two Hoover Europe "free flights" promotion programs.

The quarter ended September 30, 1992 includes a nonrecurring $95 million pretax charge relating to the reorganization of the Company's North American and European operations.

Selected Financial Data
Thousands of Dollars Except Per Share Data

	1993 (1)	1992 (2)	1991	1990	1989(3)
Net sales	$2,987,054	$3,041,223	$2,970,626	$3,056,833	$3,088,753
Cost of sales	2,262,942	2,339,406	2,254,221	2,309,138	2,312,645
Income taxes	38,600	15,900	44,400	60,500	75,500
Income (loss) from continuing operations	51,270	(8,354)	79,017	98,905	131,472
Percent of income (loss) from continuing operations to net sales	1.7%	(.3%)	2.7%	3.2%	4.3%
Income (loss) from continuing operations per share	$ .48	$ (.08)	$ .75	$ .94	$ 1.27
Dividends paid per share	.50	.50	.50	.95	.95
Average shares outstanding (in thousands)	106,252	106,077	105,761	105,617	103,694
Working capital	$ 406,181	$ 452,626	$ 509,025	$ 612,802	$ 650,905
Depreciation of property, plant and equipment	102,459	94,032	83,352	76,836	68,077
Additions to property, plant and equipment	99,300	129,891	143,372	141,410	127,838
Total assets	2,469,498	2,501,490	2,535,068	2,586,541	2,436,319
Long-term debt	724,695	789,232	809,480	857,941	876,836
Total debt to capitalization	60.6%	58.7%	45.9%	47.7%	50.6%
Shareowners' equity per share of Common stock	$ 5.50	$ 5.62	$ 9.50	$ 9.60	$ 8.89

(1) Includes $60.4 million in pretax charges ($50 million in a special charge and $10.4 million in selling, general and administrative expenses) for additional costs associated with two Hoover Europe "free flights" promotion programs.
(2) Includes a $95 million pretax charge relating to the reorganization of the North American and European business units and before cumulative effect of accounting changes.
(3) These amounts reflect the acquisition of Hoover on January 26, 1989.

Market and Dividend Information

	Sales Price of Common Shares in Whole Dollars				Dividends Per Share	
	1993		1992		1993	1992
Quarter	High	Low	High	Low		
First	$16	$13	$20	$15	$.125	$.125
Second	16	13	21	16	.125	.125
Third	18	15	18	13	.125	.125
Fourth	19	15	16	13	.125	.125

Form 10-K as filed with the Securities and Exchange Commission will be provided free of charge to our shareowners by writing to E. James Bennett, Secretary, Maytag Corporation, 403 West Fourth Street North, Newton, Iowa 50208.

Maytag Corporation Common stock is traded under the symbol MYG on the New York Stock Exchange.

Dividend Reinvestment and Stock Purchase Plan
Maytag Corporation has a program that allows shareowners to reinvest their dividends in additional shares of Common stock. Also, shareowners may make voluntary monthly investments to increase their holdings. Information on these programs is available through Shareowner Services Department, Maytag Corporation, 403 West Fourth Street North, Newton, Iowa 50208 (515-792-8000).